Mess to Majestic

A true story of recovery and healing from trauma, shame, and addictions with Biblical and clinical insights.

By Laura McCarthy, MA, LMHC, MCAP

Cover Photo by Fabrice Villard on Unsplash
Cover Design by Laura McCarthy and Nikki Helton
Editor: Beacon Point Services
Restoring Hope Publishing

Table of Contents

Chapter Six: Modern-Day Miracle

Chapter Seven: Journey of Transformative Healing and Recovery

Chapter Eight: Saved Majestic Masterpiece

Bibliography

Dedication

This book is dedicated to my mom: the most regal, resilient, and responsible parent a daughter could ever have. Not only did you overcome many trials during a time in history that was cruel and shaming for single moms and divorcees, but you thrived. You've always shown incredible fortitude and drive, gaining victory over hardship and accomplishing so much for your family. You are a picture of generosity and love I hold dear, and I will forever be grateful for your endurance, never-ending forgiveness, and unconditional love! I love you, Mom! There's no one like you! You're the best!

When God made you, the angels stood in awe and declared, "We've never seen one like that before." And they never will again! You are heaven's first and final attempt at you. You are matchless, unprecedented, and unequaled. Consequently, you can do something no one else can do in a way no one else can. Call it what you wish. A talent. A skill set. A gift. An anointing. A divine spark. An unction. A call.

Scripture says, "The Spirit has given each of us a special way of serving others" (1 Cor. 12:7). Each of us—not some of us, a few of us or the elite among us. Many people settle for someone else's story and they never find their call. Don't make the same mistake. Your existence isn't accidental. Your skills are not incidental. God has shaped each person in turn! And that includes you.

Your Uniqueness
By Max Lucado
July 1 Devotional: God with You Every Day

Acknowledgments

To my husband, Chuck: Thank you for all your patient unconditional love, support, prayers, and encouragement. You are the first human being who just wanted to *be* with me, and for no other reason than to love me, which has brought me more healing than words could ever express. Thank you for allowing God to use you to heal my heart and restore my belief in myself and humanity again. You are my greatest gift! Thank you for 30 years of amazing unconditional love and grace.

To my children, Bubba and Sugarbear: You have watched me grow from being a fear-driven, controlling, immature, parent, to a more mature, trusting, healthy adult. I'm still a work in progress. You both have outgrown me in grace, maturity, and love. You amaze me and I love you both more than all the beaver tails and ski hills God could create!

To my best friend, Patty: Thank you for all the years of listening, crying, praying, encouraging, and growing in the likeness and image of our Heavenly Father, from child to adult. Thank you for the partnership of maturing and growing up together in Christ and recovery.

To the #MeToo movement: Thank you for breaking the silence, bringing awareness to the silent suffering of untold millions and offering a space in time to be real and heal the pain of sexual abuse.

To the National Task Force movement: Thank you for working hard on breaking the stigma and disgrace of substance use disorders, for giving a platform for professionals to learn more about addictions, and for giving opportunities for recovering people to share their stories of success and healing. Recovery, healing, and hope are possible for those of us living with this chronic, deadly disease, one day at a time.

To all the twelve-step groups, Christian ministries, home church families, and friends who have been my surrogate mothers, fathers, sisters and brothers, all these years: Thank you! God has used your wisdom, direction, and love to transform my life, and the lives of my children for decades to come. We are creating a new legacy with your help and the help of God.

Last but not least, to the lover of my soul, my good Heavenly Father, my fellow sufferer, servant, and friend, Jesus Christ; and the great comforter, the Holy Spirit: thank you for loving me first. You never gave up on me. You've always been with me. Thank you that I can witness and testify to your great love. You are my great pursuer and my greatest pursuit. May this book bring you glory and honor, forever and ever.

Foreword

*And we know that all things work together for good to
them that love God, to them who are the called
according to HIS purpose.*

Romans 8:28

Dear Laura,

*Where do I begin? "Thank you" just doesn't seem to be enough.
How can you express the feelings a person gains from another
person that ultimately saves your life? "Grateful" seems so little,
"self-worthy" isn't quite right, and "thank you" is just a general
phrase.*

*Unconditional Love. That is what it is. God gave me your
unconditional love in any term or fashion that you wish to phrase it,
but I know that is what it is. I trust you with my heart and soul and
my mind. He sent me here and guided me to you. I have spent my
whole life never feeling secure or safe enough to talk to anyone
about my fears and the horrors that I endured. Then there you were.
I don't understand it myself, but I started releasing it, feeling calm
about it and being able to look you in the eyes without shame or
indignity.*

*God put us here for a reason and you were mine. In a matter of a
month, you helped me release a lifetime of turmoil. I want you to
understand that what you have done for me can never be repaid or
truly expressed in words. Saving my life in a way you may not
understand, but I think maybe you do.*

*God does create miracles and I have thanked Him that you are one
of those miracles. Because of your loving ways and kind heart, He
may have just created another miracle in me.*

*So if it means anything to you, for what it is worth, anytime you are
down or just having a bad day remember that this once hopeless,
lost soul, and desperate alcoholic truly gives you his unconditional
love.*

Past Client

Introduction

*I will give thanks to you, Lord, with all my heart; I will
tell of all your wonderful deeds. I will be glad and
rejoice in you; I will sing the praises of your name, O
most High.*

Psalm 9:1–2

For the first 25 years of my life, I stuffed shameful secrets, trauma, and pain I experienced from being a child of an addicted parent and enduring domestic violence, sexual abuse, abandonment, loss, grief, and eventually my own addictions.

My life was careening off the cliff of disaster, as I suffered in a silence that swallowed me whole and held me captive from generational patterns and strongholds that nearly destroyed my life.

But God dramatically came into my life and not only saved me but restored all the years the locusts had eaten (Joel 2:25–26), restoring life, dignity, worth, and purpose. For the past 35 years, He has taken me on a healing journey from a hardened, avoidant, chaotic, and addicted atheist to an involved, intimate, compassionate, relational human being, growing in love with God and others. With the help of empathetic and compassionate communities, therapists, educators, and God, complex chains of silence, shame, bitterness, rage, depression, anxiety, and addictions have been broken.

I've written this book intentionally combining vulnerable confessions about my vast brokenness—describing types of trauma, addictions, and shame that infected my life—with a glimpse of some of today's top clinical and biblical insights.

My call is to restore hope to the hopeless; that is what I hope this book will accomplish by informing, impacting, and inspiring others to commence their journeys of healing and recovery.

My journey from atheist to believer, from mess to majestic is really about the power of a loving God who never allows pain to go to waste. He is using it now! He loves to heal hardened hearts. There's no circumstance God finds impossible. He is the God who loves to restore hope to the hopeless.

Healing and recovery are like peeling an onion; even for me, all these years later, the onion continues to peel. When I first sat down to write this book, unresolved pain began to surface, and I was reminded once again that there's no "done button" to healing. With a humbled heart, I returned to counseling for eight months before I could pick up the pen again and resume the assignment I felt God had placed on my heart.

The layout of this book is simple. First, I'll focus on the problem—the Mess—the brokenness in my own life and my family of origin. I hope this will awaken your awareness and identification, as I believe these are keys to the beginning of transformation.

Then I draw on many of my favorite authors and ministry leaders who I consider God's instruments of healing. These insights are designed to educate and equip the reader with practical tools and hope.

Some of my readers may identify with some of the tragedies in my story and it may trigger unresolved pain. A trigger is a strong emotional reaction that can be an unexpected, subconscious pain button. You might be tempted to think this is "bad news" but the truth is "great news!"

"How?" you might ask.

The process of healing never feels good. But God allows these unresolved issues to trigger you so you will turn to Him, seek help, and dump your burden so there's more room for Him in your life and your heart.

Deeply I believe that every circumstance we go through in this life is an opportunity to draw closer to God. One of His greatest desires is to have a dynamic, loving relationship with us, and us with Him that we might in turn share that love with others. Our junk is a barrier to those relationships.

Do not judge the appearance of this pain, for from it can spring a whole new you! You may be tempted to scream, cry or run; please, be encouraged! You are on the right track—stick with it! You're worth it, even if you don't feel like it yet.

Healing isn't about forgetting, but about remembering with less pain.

This book is for anyone interested in learning more about trauma, shame, addictions, grief, and God. It's for anyone willing to do the hard work of healing, even if it means letting someone else into the story and risking trusting again. It's for anyone willing to practice seeking out safe places with safe people—including God—to talk, feel, and grieve.

If that's not you, would you consider passing this book along to others? My prayer is that anyone who reads this story will gain insight regarding the struggles they're having and they will discover there's a God who loves them, as well as many paths for healing. Most importantly, they will come away knowing there is hope for the hopeless.

Chapter One: The Mess

*Remember, O Lord, your great mercy and love for
they're from of old. Remember not the sins of my
youth and my rebellious ways: according to your love
remember me, for you are good, O Lord.*

Psalm 25:6–7

High School: Unhealthy Dependencies

Have you ever loved someone so much that you thought you
couldn't breathe without them? That's how I felt about my high
school sweetheart. He was my first love. When I met him at 16, in
my sophomore year, I was a shell of a person looking for love, and
subconsciously, I believed that if I found the right guy, he would be
the fix I needed.

Being the child of an alcoholic, I reeked of dysfunction, and I
suffered from codependency, the family disease of addiction. Both
my sweetheart and I were misfits, but together we found our
solution. From the day we met, we were inseparable. It was a fatal
attraction. Besides being immersed in each other, we were also
heavily into drinking and drugging. Our motto was "sex, drugs, and
rock "'n' roll."

My boyfriend and I became attached at the hip. Looking back
now, I realize I was living to become who he needed me to be so I
could feel loved and accepted. This is not only the face of
codependency but emotional dependency as well.

At my core, I greatly needed approval and love but that was
mixed with a great fear of rejection and abandonment. My ability to
trust someone had been shattered long ago. So I functioned from a

place of, "What could I get?" I lived from the outside in to gain approval, acceptance, and love. My well was empty. It would be years before I would understand the plight I suffered.

By my junior year, I was living a total double life. I'd been kicked out of school three times, faced expulsion, had a few run-ins with police, survived an overdose of some nasty drugs, pissed off several friends and teachers, and suffered from a bad case of insecurity and rebellion.

On the other hand, even while skipping school, I managed above-average grades; excelled at fine arts; played the violin; taught myself the guitar and springboard diving, which landed me a position on the varsity swim team; and was headed towards a professional skiing career. I was fiercely competitive and independent.

I was driven to perform out of a heart that had been crippled in childhood. I'd decided early on that I wasn't going to need anyone; being vulnerable to need was a guaranteed recipe for rejection. Maintaining complete control in this and every relationship, I lived by the motto, "Where there's a will, there's a way!"

Despite the control I maintained, I was perpetually discontented and always up for a good fight. I suffered from distorted beliefs about self, men, women, life, and God, all of which were set up in my family of origin, going back generations. This isn't a statement of blame; it's just a fact. As my friend Karin would say, "What I experienced in my childhood has affected my whole life."

After a year of crazy, we broke up. To say I felt devastated would be an understatement. I had taken a risk with love, or at least what I thought was love, and it had not paid off. My heart slammed shut. Hopeless despair and feelings of complete and total worthlessness reemerged.

The relationship had only been a cover-up for my lack of sense of self and subzero self-esteem. It had become my only sense of identity. He had gone, and what little esteem I had felt was gone with him. I think a codependent's first love relationship is like an alcoholic's first drink: one they'll never forget.

Diving deeper into the abyss of darkness, I played the field, got drunk and high, and spun completely out of control with no thought or care for anyone, including myself. I was hard-hearted and hopeless. I was using men, alcohol, drugs—pretty much anything I could get my hands on. But they say God loves drunks and fools, and I believe my survival is proof.

My school party buddies and I formed a drinking group called the 151 Club. We even designed and sandblasted matching glasses in the shop class. My drinking and drugging had reached a whole new level of despicable, though, and soon got me ousted. I had become unpredictable at best, and my friends dropped like flies. Rejection followed me like a stray dog.

During this time, my mom sent me off to live with my alcoholic father (I'll discuss this more later). Suffice it to say things got worse, not better, and I came back home worse than ever.

My mom had remarried when I was 12. On more than one occasion, my stepfather greeted me at the door with an Alka-Seltzer and a glass of water, treating my under-age drunkenness like a comedy act. He did not seem to mind my drinking but swore if I ever got caught with drugs, he'd personally call the local sheriff. I went to extra measures to hide my drugs.

My mom, on the other hand, was fed up. At the end of my senior year of high school, she offered me two choices: take the car, leave, and never come home again; or go to college immediately after high school and stay there year-round.

College Years: Oblivion

Being relatively smart, I took the car-and-college option, so eight days after high school graduation (which in itself had been nothing short of a miracle), I was dropped off at my college dorm on the campus of Washington State University. Within a few days, I found my people; I rarely drew a sober breath my entire college career. I was lost in a sea of oblivion.

As a user and a taker, it was all a game, and people were just my objects, giving me attention, approval, acceptance, drugs, sex, and alcohol. I blew through so many relationships. Today, I hear the term "friends with benefits," but honestly, I did not get close enough to anyone to be called their friend. I just wanted all the benefits without the relationship, the whole time starving for connection and belonging. I was an empty well of need, seductively seeking something or someone to fill the void.

Danger to Self and Others

As recovering people, we often look back on our lives and marvel at the situations we survived during our drinking and drugging days. I skirted death more than once, and I do thank God daily for surviving my insanity. I praise Him for protecting so many potential innocent victims.

In 1978, the legal drinking age in Washington State was 21; just over the border in Moscow, home of the University of Idaho, it was 19. My roommate would loan me her ID so I could falsify my age at 18 and bar-hop in Idaho. I can remember covering one eye to drive back home with double vision on more than one occasion, oblivious to risk or danger.

According to state statistics, the 15-minute stretch of road that linked the two universities was the most dangerous highway. It was known as Dead Man's Alley. More drunk-driving accidents happened on that stretch of road than any other. This humbles me every day now I'm sober and clean; to think I survived this drive many times so wasted I could barely walk to the car, let alone drive. Such behavior could certainly be called insanity.

One haunting memory from this period occurred during a trip to the hydro boat races. Driving in my VW Bug, drunk, with three passengers, I carelessly passed a semi-truck, playing chicken with another coming the other way. My occupants screamed in terror, but I callously blamed their fear on their lack of faith in my superior driving ability. I squeaked by both semis with barely a second to spare.

I suffered from a sickening, deadly denial that blinded my reasoning. Today, I give God all the credit for our survival, but at this time in my story, God was only a curse word in my vocabulary, not a real person or a living power.

The return trip home that weekend was lonely. No one dared get back in my car. I blew them off; it was their problem, or so I thought. My attitude was "Who cares!" I devalued and discounted others' negative comments about my drinking and driving.

My college years are a blur of achievements and failures. Being an overachiever, I lived my life high on my accomplishments and I was always doing. I acted in a key role in the university's main stage production of *The Crucible* and worked multiple jobs: ballet instructor, ski patroller, ski-lift operator, photo editor for one of the largest yearbooks per capita in the US, campus tour guide, bookkeeper, and hostess for a local restaurant.

Due to my excessive lifestyle, my college attendance was spotty at best. My grades declined, I got busted for smoking pot in the dorm, and I rapidly lost roommates and relationships, as well as my credibility and integrity. I don't even think those words were in my vocabulary yet.

I succeeded in trashing and burning respect, relationships and reliability. I didn't make friends; I took hostages. With my progressing addictions, my life revolved around staying busy, attempting to fill the aching void within my soul. I felt like a human vacuum cleaner, sucking up everything in my path—but I had a hole in my bag. I was insatiable.

Clinical Insights: What Is Codependency?

> Nothing can be more demoralizing than a clinging and abject dependence upon another human being. This often amounts to the demand for a degree of protection and love that no one could possibly satisfy. So our hoped-for protectors finally flee and once more we are left alone—either to grow up or disintegrate.

Bill W, Cofounder of AA (Alcoholics Anonymous World Services Inc., 1967)

The term *codependent* was coined in the 70s from the clinical community when professionals began to identify co-addicts or codependents: family members and/or friends closest to the chemically dependent persons who were struggling with symptoms similar to those arising from the disease of addiction. Instead of being obsessed with the chemical, for example, they were obsessed with the chemically dependent person. Codependency was then identified as the family disease of addiction.

Today, I broaden the definition of the term codependency to include anyone who gives their power away to someone or something else to define their value. It's letting outside influences determine your worth. When we fall into this pattern, we call that a slip into codependency.

Coming from a family of addiction, individuals can show a clear pattern of maladaptive and/or unhealthy behaviors that include protecting and covering up for their loved one, lying, caretaking, and worrying—all at the expense of their own lives or livelihood, and all in the name of love. Codependents' lives become completely centered around the addict. They turn into super protectors and providers, in the hope that the behavior they call "love" will bring the addict out of their addiction, allowing them to return to make a happy home, relationship, or life.

Unfortunately, the opposite outcome would occur as the codependent regressed into the insanity of trying multiple methods to manipulate, fix, control, enable, or manage the disease. Very much like the progression of chemical addiction, codependents became emotionally and physically sicker, harboring fierce resentments, fear, and despair. The harder they try to beat the addiction of the addict, the sicker they become.

One of the saddest stories I heard while working in the treatment field was about a middle-aged mother whose young adult son was incarcerated for his substance use disorder. To the outside observer, she had a beautiful life: a career, a home, and a future. Yet she struggled with severe codependency. She was so enmeshed with her son and his progressive disease that she took on his shame and failures as her own. Shortly after he was incarcerated, she took her own life, unable to bear the shame and pain. In other words, she met the same destructive end as many chemically dependent persons without treatment: death.

Family members who have reached their wits' end plead with professionals to help their addicted loved ones. At this point, a referral to treatment for the whole family is vital. Many are shocked at the suggestion; they believe that the chemically dependent person is the only one with the problem, not them.

As a therapist, I'd ask one fundamental question to explore the depth of codependency: "How much of your day is spent thinking about your addicted loved one?" Typically, the response is 90 to 100 percent; they're preoccupied, obsessed even, with the life and safety of another. This is the essence of codependency.

As the disease progresses, denial blocks their ability to see the truth. Their obsession and codependency cause them to take on more and more responsibilities, and they begin to live the other person's life—to the point of abandoning their own.

For the children of addicted parents, this can become a full role reversal; a hideous form of child abuse, where the child feels responsible for the adult. The child takes on more and more adult responsibilities, becoming self-parented. The family disease of addiction causes immense impact and suffering. Left untreated, the codependent careens down a path of losses: livelihood, finances, sense of self, freedom, and ultimately life itself.

Treatment and education can begin the process of smashing denial. Attending twelve-step groups also helps break the cycle of anxiety, and shame. Al-Anon Family Groups—twelve-step groups for the families and friends of alcoholics—birthed the three Cs and the three As. "You didn't *Cause* the disease. You can't *Control* the disease. You can't *Cure* the disease" (Al-Anon Family Groups, ND).

There's a God, and I am not He. God's power is the only

power that can pull people back from the path that leads to insanity and/or death. *Awareness, Acceptance,* and *Action* are valuable principles instilled in Al-Anon Family Groups that can aid in recovery and self-care.

There's another principle that can help. The *hula hoop theory* helps people set boundaries which are life-saving. It goes like this: Imagine yourself stepping into a hula hoop. The other person is stepping into their hula hoop. Everything in your hula hoop is your business. Everything in the other person's hula hoop is their business. To recover and heal from codependency, the focus has to be on self. Simply put: if it's not in your hula hoop, it's none of your business. The Bible says *"make it your ambition to lead a quiet life, and mind your own business..."* (1 Thes. 4:11). In other words, stay in your own hula hoop.

Learning whose responsibilities are whose is vitally important because as the disease of addiction progresses, the addicted person becomes less and less responsible and the codependent person and/or family system will pick up more and more responsibility, blame, and shame.

I often use the oxygen mask analogy to hit this principle home. If I'm flying on an airplane with my child next to me and the oxygen masks come down, whose mask do I put on first? Mine or my child's? This isn't a trick question. Nine out of ten times, clients will say "the child." Unfortunately, this is the wrong answer. The correct answer is *you*! You are *first*. Many times, great resistance rises at this answer and I hear, "That's selfish!"

My answer? "No. That's self-caring." To reframe the issue: If a person doesn't take care of themselves first, then they will not be available to love and raise that child. We must learn to put on our oxygen mask first. Save your own life, and then your child's. Self-care has to be *first*. Learning to take care of your responsibilities and trust the other person to take care of theirs is a basic rule of boundary setting. If the person is old enough to do it for themselves, let them.

There's one dilemma with this idea. When the codependent person starts to practice self-caring behavior and shifts the focus to self, an earthquake-level anxiety will be unleashed. A simple look at neuroscience can explain this physical reaction, because codependency is a behavioral addiction.

Clinical Insights: the Neuroscience of Behavioral Addictions

Patterns of repetitive behavior build pathways in the brain. Familiar pathways can be built from worrying, caretaking, enabling, rescuing, fixing, covering up, and/or protecting. Let's imagine your addict calls you, and your maladaptive behaviors immediately kick in like some kind of autopilot. It's habitual—a pattern of repeated responses.

Your brain pathways are built on repetitive, habitual behavioral and/or emotional responses, and become dependent on them. It could be any type of repetitive response built over time: rescuing, playing victim, feeling anger, manipulating, caretaking, self-pity. In other words, any maladaptive or unhealthy coping mechanism.

So let's say you come into recovery and/or treatment. You've been unaware of these subconscious pathways, but now you begin to see that you're in a pattern of crisis and rescue, crisis and rescue. And let's say you're given an assignment to do self-care and stop rescuing.

You're practicing the new self-caring behaviors when one day the crisis hits. You're no longer supposed to be fixing or rescuing your loved one. Suddenly you become aware of new, intense feelings of anxiety and crazy. Your brain is going into withdrawal from its familiar codependent behavior.

Your old pathways are programmed to *fix, rescue,* and *caretake.* They're screaming at you, *"Fold, cave in, go back to the familiar. Fix! Rescue! Caretake!"* To cave in will bring relief as the old brain pathways get their fix—but recovery requires you to do just the opposite. This never feels good. I often warn new clients that it's going to feel worse before it gets better.

Like any addiction, recovery from codependency is very difficult. Building new pathways in the brain will take time and work, and sometimes extra help is necessary. Unfortunately, many go back to old behaviors to calm their anxiety rather than walking through the pain of starving the old pathways and building new ones with healthier habits.

It is called care*taking* for a reason. The subconscious motive isn't giving or loving, although most people claim they love their addict, and many believe it is true love, it's not. The underlying motive is to fill the void and/or pain, to avoid withdrawal; that isn't caregiving, but care*taking.* Check your motives. If you're able to be gut-level honest with yourself or others, you will begin to break the cycle.

Codependents face two choices: stay stuck in the drama, trauma, blame, shame and isolation game, and continue downward into despair and hopelessness; or seek treatment, therapy, and/or a support group to begin the process of change and healing.

Isolation and shame are twin traits of the family disease of addiction. Shame locks the sufferer into isolation, and no one ever grows in isolation. The dysfunctional family rules fall into place. "Don't talk. Don't trust. Don't feel."

Overcoming this disease without support is virtually impossible because withdrawal and temptation are so powerful. A person needs support and accountability to build a new life, free to focus and care for self in healthy and affirming, life-building ways. You can't use a broken brain to fix a broken life.

Clinical Insights: the Power of WE

Support groups have grown in popularity and success for many reasons. They can be safe places where sufferers can find others who have struggled and have gained victory over their old ways of dealing with relationships and life. People tend to share suggestions or tools they've used to overcome their old dysfunctional or maladaptive patterns of feeling and/or behaving.

Those who have been in recovery for a while can offer understanding and empathy. People who share experiences with them can find belonging, validation, accountability, and acceptance. Their message is simple and powerful: you are not alone! There's something you can do. It takes work, and you are worth it.

The power of *we* is the power of empathy, compassion, and understanding which builds hope and belonging. These qualities are also helpful in healing shame and isolation.

Support groups can also be a place to learn new tools for self-care. The healthy new you can learn boundaries, assertive communication skills, how to detach with love and let go, and a whole host of other tools. Here is one of my favorites.

Letting go

To let go does not mean to stop caring, it means I can't
do it for someone else.

To let go isn't to cut myself off, it's the realization I
can't control another.

To let go isn't to enable, but to allow learning from
natural consequences.

To let go is to admit powerlessness, which means the
outcome isn't in my hands.

To let go isn't to try to change or blame another, it's to
make the most of myself.

To let go isn't to care for, but to care about.

To let go isn't to fix, but to be supportive.

To let go isn't to judge, but to allow another to be a
human being.

To let go isn't to be protective, it's to permit another
to face reality.

To let go isn't to deny, but to accept.

To let go isn't to regret the past, but to grow and live
for the future.

To let go is to fear less and love more.

(author unknown)

For where two or three gather in my name, there am I
with them.

Matthew 18:20

Biblical Insights: the Power of God and Spiritual Attachment

Let Go and Let God, as the *Alcoholics Anonymous* slogan says. But this is a foreign concept for many people, both in and out of recovery. "Trust the process. One day at a time," people would say in meetings. Often a confession would be heard around the room: "I have trust issues."

Trusting does not come naturally. In most cases, the trust of addicted individuals has been betrayed or grossly violated. Many beginners start to relearn trust by watching others in twelve-step meetings. We most often learn about trusting and relying upon God from the stories others share on their journey of building faith. Going to meetings helps us begin to break the isolation, loneliness and shame patterns, but also allows us to hear and see how others have learned to trust again.

When the disease of addiction runs rampant in a person's life, trust is destroyed on multiple levels. Learning and building trust is a process; trust is built—not just given. In the beginning, most people have to learn new ways to build trust with themselves, others, and God.

One unique thing about the twelve-step model of recovery is that no one dictates what anyone else believes. Instead, it asks one question: Are you willing to believe? This question opened up the door of faith for me and many others.

The second step in the twelve-step model says that we "came to believe that a power greater than ourselves could restore us to sanity." There's still much more insanity to come in my story ... but for now, let me introduce the idea of *secure attachment*. It's where we find someone safe who can meet all our needs.

When we come out of alcoholic, addicted, or dysfunctional families, we suffer from an insecure attachment. We don't know who to trust or whether we can trust. That was my experience. But after years of searching and trying to fill the void in my life alone, I found the one person and power in the universe that is intentionally, perfectly, and lovingly interested in meeting all our needs. In the AA text they say, "that one is God, may you find Him now." (Alcoholics Anonymous World Services, Inc, 2001)

In the Bible, He is described as our fortress, a secure place where all our needs are met.

> *The Lord is my rock, my fortress, and my deliverer; my*
> *God is my rock, in whom I take refuge, my shield, and*
> *the horn of my salvation, my stronghold.*

Psalm 18:2

Learning to trust and lean on God to meet all our needs is part of spiritual growth. As we grow in our knowledge of the truth of God, we can grow in belief and trust, and eventually rest. This is the journey of growing in faith.

For me, a vital spiritual experience began when I became willing to believe that maybe everything I thought about God was wrong. That, despite all my painful experiences in this life, there was still a good God who could offer me a true secure attachment. He could be the one person I could completely depend on.

Through all my years of trials and struggles, I have found He has offered Himself consistently as a replacement for my loneliness and insecurity. He has become a safe and secure place—a fortress. Listen to some of the promises found in Psalm 23:

The Lord is my Shepherd	He offers relationships day and night.
I shall not want	He shall supply all your needs!
He maketh me to lie down in green pastures	He offers rest!
He leadeth me beside the still waters	He will refresh us!
He restoreth my soul	He is the great healer!
He leadeth me in the paths of righteousness	He will guide and direct my path!
For His name sake	Gives my life purpose!
Yea, though I walk through the valley of the shadow of death	Life is difficult. I will walk through the valley of the shadow of death, but God is with me.
I will fear no evil	He offers protection.
For Thou art with me	He is faithfully present and by my side.
Thy rod and Thy staff they comfort me	He provides safe boundaries that comfort.
Thou preparest a table before me in the presence of my enemies	He offers hope in spite of my circumstances!
Thou anointest my head with oil	We are anointed and sealed with His Spirit; chosen, forgiven, righteous, approved of, loved, and significant.
My cup runneth over	He offers us an abundant table to sit at.
Surely goodness and mercy shall follow me all the days of my life	His grace, His power, His plan will rule over our life. That's Blessing!
And I will dwell in the house of the Lord Forever!	We are secure! *Now and into All Eternity!*

I was a complete skeptic in the beginning. Yet over time, and through multiple experiences which I will share later in this book, God has shown up and has met all my needs. He offers to meet your needs, too, now and forever. He will meet your needs for provision, worth, significance, security, belonging, approval, acceptance, and so much more. He doesn't have grandchildren. We are all his children. He created us and knows exactly what we need. Maybe you don't know this God? Well, hang on! That's what this book is about: Introducing you to the One who loves you and can heal every part of your life.

Chapter Two: Death, Loss, and Grief

I will not die; instead I will live to tell what the Lord has done for me.

Psalm 118:17

After graduating from college in three and a half years, I returned to a furnished duplex my parents owned. The previous year, my former high school sweetheart had survived a violent bar attack, in which he was jumped by three guys and beaten near death. He was forever altered. Now I was back on home territory, our codependent relationship was rekindled from a spark of guilt and pity. We were back together like love bugs on a hot Florida night, with the promise of a future—ring and all.

Once again, he was my life, my future, my hope, my dreams, and my breath. All of which was about to be smashed. One night after work, I came home to find him lying on the couch complaining of a severe headache. We went to the local hospital emergency room, and the news was catastrophic: he had an inoperable brain tumor. There was nothing they could do for him. They gave him six months to live. I was 21 years old. He was 22.

Depression, Drinking, Drugging, and Hopeless Despair

In the receiving line at his memorial service a few short months later, I felt numb with disbelief and shock. Following the service, I got completely wasted and crawled around on my living room floor, cursing and crying out accusations to a God I didn't believe in. I could not reconcile the idea of a loving God with the pain of this loss. A dark cloud of depression and anger engulfed me like an unremitting winter storm.

As I settled into my cavern of darkness, my focus was entirely on my pain, my loss, my dreams. I was completely absorbed in me. My conclusion was that these terrible things had happened to me because I was so messed up and worthless—or, better yet, because God was dead. Beliefs are powerful.

The gaping hole in my soul had latched on to the idea that I would only be *someone* if someone else believed I was someone. In other words, I was because he was; now that he wasn't, I wasn't, either. Life as I knew it was over. He had been my purpose for living, so now there was no reason to live. I believed with every fiber of my being that there were three deaths that day: mine, his, and God's. These are the true lies of codependency and atheism.

My life became filled with round-the-clock parties filled with booze, drugs, and men. It was a very dark time in my young life. It was a crazy mix of unknown chemical cocktails, bars, and strangers' homes. I was lost in a sea of mind-numbing excesses. There was no thought of tomorrow—only oblivion and the need to block out all feelings of loss and despair. My life had been shattered by his death.

One night as I was feeding my cravings, smothering my pain, I totaled my stepdad's truck in a drunken blackout. It was a miracle I was driving his truck and not my VW Bug, which was sitting in the mechanic's shop, having thrown a rod the previous week. These are what I call divine appointments; if I had been driving my car, I might not be here telling this story.

I was fortunate in another way, too: the driving under the influence (DUI) ticket got diverted because the campus police knew my stepfather and held the city police at bay while they served me a negligent driving ticket.

It was during this distraught, depressive period that my deceased beloved's mother came into my home and took all of his possessions except for a small picture of Jesus and an old fishing rod. On the counter, she left a card bearing this Bible verse.

Praise be to the God and Father of our Lord Jesus Christ, the Father of compassion and the God of all comfort, who comforts us in all our troubles so that we can comfort those in any trouble with the comfort we ourselves receive from God.

2 Corinthians 1:3-4.

"What a joke!" I thought. It would be years before I understood the significance of this passage.

God Is Dead

In my grief, I believed a lie: God was my enemy. I was not willing to believe this pain could or would result in anything good, nor that a good God would allow such suffering. How could a loving God allow this? It was easier for me to write God off as dead and move on.

In truth, God was very much alive. *I* was the problem. Better yet, sin was the problem. I was stuck in rage, bitterness, blame, and blasphemy. I showed contempt for God and played the part of a victim who could not accept life on His terms.

There is an undeniable fact in this life: every birth certificate comes with a death certificate. How arrogant was I to stand against the Author of life as a self-proclaimed player when I had no control over either? I was stuck in blame and therefore stuck in my pain; I stayed there for many years. I was truly a mess.

I would be remiss to say I did not have faith. Just the opposite: I had faith in my chemicals and in my Great Big

Wonderful Self. I was an egomaniac with an inferiority complex, as I've heard said. My chemicals and my ego were all I trusted.

I dove deeper into the evil, excessive lifestyle I now worshipped. Somehow I managed to get a few jobs but lost them in rapid succession. The last one landed me a severance check; it was my ticket out of Washington.

Geographical Cure

In the pit of my grief, with money in hand, I accepted an invitation to move to the Colorado high country. My old ski buddies had started the ProMogul Tour, a group of mogul snow-skiers (also known as freestylers) attempting to make money and an honest transition from ski bums to professionals. I'd grown up skiing with these guys and was already working as an instructor at one of our local mountains; I'd dreamed of competing, so this invitation sparked a new flame of hopeful determination. Without a job or a relationship to tie me down, I loaded up my VW Bug and headed east—with plenty of drugs and alcohol for the ride.

Arriving in Breckenridge, Colorado in August of 1983, I was 23 years old and felt depressed and desperately alone, but my solution—to find a man, a job, and a place to live—was in place within a week. I was good at finding men, jobs, and homes; I just couldn't keep them. The pervasive lie that governed my life at that time was that without a man, I had no worth. My life's purpose was to find a man and meet his every need or suffer the consequences. The dreaded fear of abandonment and loneliness plagued me.

The geographical cure is changing where we live, subconsciously and unknowingly taking ourselves and our problems with us. It's the false hope of a new future, as we drag all the unresolved past along with us. You can't fix a broken life with a broken life.

Clinical Insights: What Is Grief?

Life is painful! There's no way of escaping pain, loss, or grief on this side of life.

Pastor Jimmy Evans, founder and author of *Marriage on the Rock* and the *Dream Marriage* series, validates that point in *When Life Hurts*. Here are his five emotional facts of life:

1. Life hurts, period. And it is inevitable that as we age we will accumulate more hurts.
2. When we don't deal with our pain, it drops into the "Hurt Pocket," the place where hurt accumulates.
3. Accumulated pain and unresolved problems compromise our mental, emotional, spiritual, and relational health.
4. We all deal with pain in some way, right or wrong. Sometimes it comes out in the form of addiction—food, gambling, sex, drugs, or alcoholism. When this happens, the issue is never the issue. So then alcohol isn't the issue, the pain is the issue.
5. The only way to stop the hurt and resolve it is to turn it toward God; we have to empty our hurt pockets. We need to be honest before God to resolve our pain. We need to forgive ourselves and others.

(Evans, ND)

The book of Job shows us an incredible example of a man who grieved well. He laments, pouring out his heart to God for 35 chapters:

> He doubts. He questions. He gets angry. He wants to die. But he continues to engage with God, to believe in the goodness of God, even as he tries to make sense of his suffering. In the end, he is spiritually transformed and brought to a new place by the Lord, who "blessed the latter part of Job's life more than the (first)" (Job 42:12).

(Scazzero P. , 2017, p. 50)

The formulation of the stages of grief was developed by Dr. Elizabeth Kubler-Ross, one of the most widely respected professionals on the topic, in her book, *On Death and Dying:*

Kubler-Ross' first stage is **denial**. In this stage, grieving people are unable or unwilling to accept that the loss has taken (or will shortly take) place. It can feel as though they're experiencing a bad dream, that the loss is unreal, and they're waiting to "wake up" as though from a dream, expecting that things will be normal.

After people have passed through denial and accepted that the loss has occurred (or will shortly occur), they may begin to feel **anger** at the loss and the unfairness of it. They may become angry at the person who has been lost (or is dying). Feelings of abandonment may also occur.

Next comes **bargaining**. In this stage, people beg their "higher power" to undo the loss, saying things along the lines of, "I'll change if you bring her (or him) back to me." This phase usually involves promises of better behavior or significant life change which will be made in exchange for the reversal of the loss.

Once it becomes clear that anger and bargaining are not going to reverse the loss, people may then sink into a **depression** stage where they confront the inevitability and reality of the loss and their own helplessness to change it. During this period, grieving people may cry, experience sleep or eating habit changes, or withdraw from other relationships and activities while they process the loss they have sustained. People may also blame themselves for having caused or in some way contributed to their loss, whether or not this is justified.

Finally (if all goes according to Dr. Kubler-Ross's plan), people enter a stage of **acceptance** where they have processed their initial grief emotions, are able to accept that the loss has occurred and cannot be undone, and are once again able to plan for their futures and re-engage in daily life.

(Kubler-Ross, 2019)

Passing through these stages of grief is vitally important, and becoming stuck in any one stage of the grief process can cause unnecessary misery. We often hear in the recovery rooms that "Pain is inevitable, but misery is optional." It is worth learning how to grieve well and heal. Healing doesn't mean we forget; it's just remembering with less pain.

Pastor Evans goes on to say that we have to take responsibility for our pain. We are not victims and hanging on to blame and anger only keeps us stuck in the pain. But in our grief, we can feel hopeless and helpless, as Kubler-Ross describes.

We not only grieve those we've lost to death, divorce, or disease; we also grieve as adult children. We grieve for the things we never received, like healthy parenting. We lament the nurturing or affection we did not receive. Maybe we have to grieve a lack of positive and affirming words in our childhood. Perhaps we didn't have structure or boundaries, healthy communication or the sharing of wisdom, lessons learned or things to avoid. Maybe there was a loss of innocence—or worse, events that happened against your will and caused a loss of control. Whatever your loss, it benefits you to grieve it and work towards achieving acceptance.

To stay stuck in any stage of grief is to stay blocked. It shuts us off from relationships, life, love, and God. It is a darkness that can consume the soul like cancer and spread to every area of our life, and it does not go away with time. By itself, time does not heal; we must be proactive in working through our grief, or in time we can find ourselves facing depression or even hopeless despair and suicide.

As you go through this process, you must have safe people to trust and lean on. People who will allow you to be vulnerable, transparent, and real; people who can allow you the dignity of your journey, letting you cry without fixing, rescuing, or lecturing. Trustworthy, caring, and compassionate individuals and/or groups who value the grieving process, who are comfortable just being with you: true listeners, comfortable with tears and sadness.

Of course, those of faith have an even greater listener and comforter on their team: God. Not only does He offer His partnership and presence but His promises propel us to the other side of our grief. We also have a partner in our pain: Christ. He suffered as we suffered. He knows death, sorrow, and pain.

Biblical Insights: What Is Trust?

For a person with faith in God, what blossoms from the pain is belief and the trust in the power of a loving God to have the perfect plan.

> *"For I know the plans I have for you," declares the Lord, "plans to prosper you and not to harm you, plans to give you hope and a future."*

Jeremiah 29:11

As we are released from our shock and denial, we can own our grief and cry out to God.

We can begin to release our anger, bitterness, sadness, disbelief, and loss to the cross. It is there we find fellowship, forgiveness, grace, and mercy; God's love can transform our loss to love and give us hope of a better plan. This can be the beginning of acceptance and a deeper way of building trust.

> *Even though he slay me, yet will I trust him.*

Job 13:15 (KJV)

We all have faith. We all trust that when we press the switch, the light will come on. We trust that when we put the key in the ignition, the car engine will start; that if we approach a green light, the traffic on the opposite side will stop.

We all put our trust in something. So trust isn't the problem; rather, the problem is the object of our trust. Who do you trust today? Yourself? Your money, your abilities, your spouse? How about God? He is the most stable and trustworthy person on or off the planet.

It's important to understand that we are all passing through this earth. This isn't our final destination. Our final resting place is heaven, a place where we will live with the One who perfectly loves us into all eternity.

Acceptance is facing and embracing the realities of this life with grace and dignity. We must accept that we are all in the process of dying even as we live; some people prematurely require a brutal trust that enables them to rest in the certainty that God has a better plan. This is a journey of faith.

We have seasons where we build and acquire, but then we start experiencing the limitations of this life. We lose what we've acquired—our good health, personal belongings, friends, spouses, and abilities. But these losses are a part of life we all have to accept. This life is a journey of loss. If we can learn to grieve well and to completely trust our Master Healer and Great Comforter for our future, laying our lives into the arms of the Great I Am for eternity, we will benefit greatly.

In the book, *Ruthless Trust*, Brennan Manning tells a story from George Maloney's book, *In Jesus We Trust* (Notre Dame, IN Ave Maria Press, 1990, pg. 129), that describes a spiritual lesson in trust for us all.

Fourteenth-century theologian and mystic John Tauler prayed for eight years that God would send him a person who would teach him the true way of perfection. One day, while at prayer, he heard a voice from within telling him to go outside to the steps of the church and there he would meet his mentor. He obeyed without hesitation. On the church steps, Tauler found a barefoot ragamuffin in rags, wounded and caked in blood.

Tauler greeted the man cordially. "Good morning, dear brother. May God give you a good day and grant you a happy life."

"Sir," replied the ragamuffin. "I do not remember ever having a bad day."

Stunned, Tauler asked him how that was possible since sadness and grief are part of the human condition.

The beggar explained, "You wished me a good day and I replied that I cannot recall ever having spent a bad day. You see, whether my stomach is full or I am famished with hunger, I praise God equally; when I am rebuffed and despised I still thank God. My trust in God's providence and His plan for my life is absolute, so there's no such thing as a bad day."

He continued, "Sir, you also wished me a happy life. I must insist that I am always happy, for it would be untruthful to state otherwise. My experience of God has taught me that whatever He does, must of necessity be good. Thus everything that I receive from His loving hand or whatever He permits me to receive from the hands of others – be it prosperity or adversity, sweet or bitter – I accept with joy and see it the sign of his favor. For many years now my first resolution each morning is to attach myself to nothing but the will of God alone. I have learned that the will of God is the love of God. And by the outpouring of His grace, I have so merged my will with His that whatever He wills, I will too. Therefore I've always been happy."

The beggar's witness to Jesus Christ lay in ruthless trust in the love of God and in the determination "for all things give thanks" (1 Thes. 5:18). Later in his life, Tauler wrote that "this amalgam of trust and gratitude is the shortest path to God."

(Manning, *Ruthless Trust*, 2002, pp. 162-163)

This is an amazing faith: to trust that no matter what is happening in this life, God knows and is present to walk us through it. To help those who are in the process of grieving today, I invite you to say this prayer:

Lord, as I pass through the season of grief, please help me acknowledge the pain of the loss, and pass through the stages of grief without getting stuck in any one stage, especially blame, anger, bitterness, depression or revenge. Help me pass through each stage of grief with dignity and grace. Help me release the destructive power of this loss into the cross, and receive your healing power of righteousness, freedom, and joy. Help me see any lies the enemy may be shooting at my heart during this time, and bind my mind to your truth, that you are good, and that despite these losses, you have a good plan. Help me trust you in spite of my circumstances and feelings. Thank you that you love me and are present here to comfort me during this grief. Someday, help me turn this grief and loss into an opportunity to comfort and help others as your word promises. Until then, hold me close and make your love and comfort known to me and all those who are sharing in this loss. Thank you, Lord. In Jesus' name I pray, Amen.

Chapter Three: Lessons from an Alcoholic Father—Messy!

Who has woe? Who has sorrow? Who has strife? Who has complaints? Who has needless bruises? Who has bloodshot eyes? Those who linger over wine, who go to sample bowls of mixed wine. Do not gaze at wine when it is red, when it sparkles in the cup when it goes down smoothly! In the end, it bites like a snake and poisons like a viper. Your eyes will see strange sights and your mind imagine confusing things. You will be like one sleeping on the high seas, lying on top of the rigging. "They hit me," you will say, "but I'm not hurt! They beat me, but I don't feel it! When will I wake up so I can find another drink?"

Prov. 23:29–35

Abandoned at Birth

In 1958, my 16-year-old mother was living in northern California when my very attractive 19-year-old father moved in and became the boy next door. He stole my mother's heart and swept her off her feet. The following year, she became pregnant with me. He did the right thing and married her, but his parents convinced him we were "not good enough" for him, and he left us before I was born, in the spring of 1960. Unbeknownst to anyone, he was already in the early stages of alcoholism.

My mom went through a lot of chaos and turmoil during her pregnancy, besides her abandonment by my father. Her mother, after 32 years of marriage, started an affair with a younger man. There were brief episodes of domestic violence between them where my mother would be called in to rescue, but despite every attempt, my grandmother still left her marriage and family.

I can only imagine the level of pain, anxiety, and anger my mom felt from these losses. She was only 18 years old but showed incredible courage and resilience and she bounced back quickly. Baby in tow, she went through with divorcing my dad and later married another man, promising to care for his two children while he cared for us.

When I was two, my biological father came back in the picture and convinced my mom that she was the only woman he had ever truly loved; he could not live without her. There's so much power in first love. And so the story goes that they flew to Mexico, and my mom got divorced and remarried the same day. The happy family was reunited.

Alcoholism: A Progressive Family Disease

Unfortunately, the truth was that my father's alcoholism had progressed and he was now sicker than ever. At 22 years old, he committed vehicular homicide in a drunk-driving accident, killing his passenger and running his head through a guard rail. He sustained over 250 stitches across his forehead, skull, and down his back; he also lost his spleen, greatly diminishing his alcohol tolerance.

I believe the unhealed shame of this accident, coupled with the feelings of worthlessness from his childhood, fueled his chronic progressive illness, alcoholism; notice I say fueled, not caused. Many people growing up in healthy, functional homes will later develop the disease of alcoholism, so trauma is not the cause—but it does increase the risk. I'll give you more data on this later in the chapter.

My father seemed stern, angry, and punishing. The story of Dr. Jekyll and Mr. Hyde describes my experience well; I never knew who to expect. Would he be the loving father I craved or the mean, drunk father I feared? I felt extremely insecure. I can remember experiencing comfort a few times, but more often than not, I was being punished in ways that caused me to feel an incredible amount of fear and shame.

My mother's father told me years later he never liked the way my dad treated me. He validated my pain. My grandfather knew the pain of an alcoholic father: his father, my great-grandfather, had been a very mean, angry alcoholic. He eventually died of gangrene from excessive drinking and smoking as they medically amputated his limbs from his feet to his groin before he finally passed. Drunks die dirty little deaths.

Fear and loneliness were my constant companions as a child. Being an only child, I mostly played alone in the garage or out on the front sidewalk with my skates or bike. My father worked and was gone a lot. When he was home, I was filled with roof-shaking anxiety.

There was an absence of positive words or comfort in our home; I felt cold and empty most of the time. Maybe we were all in a state of survival. (There is no blame in this statement, just the reality of a family system suffering from the progressive illness of alcoholism, a slow decline of security and well-being.)

I will share a couple of incidents with my father that fortified my terror and shame. When I was five, I remember riding in the back seat of a car that resembled an old 1950 Chevy Bel Air. I was scrunched up in the corner of the back seat, crying. My father was driving while furiously attempting to grab me.

Squirming to disappear between the crack of the seat and passenger door, I was trapped and terrorized. He finally got a hold of my collar, yanked me up to his angry face and yelled, "Stop crying or I'll give you something to cry about!" Then, just as abruptly, he threw me back into my corner. On the spot, the tears stopped. Shock set in. My feelings were frozen within me for years.

At seven, my mom bought me a beagle puppy; her name was Suzy. She was a brown-and-white short-haired beauty, and I was so excited. It's the first time in my life I remember feeling love and joy. I took her everywhere: show and tell, school, to bed. We were inseparable. I loved that puppy.

One afternoon, Dad came home drunk and angry. My parents got into a huge fight. He stormed out of the house. Suzy and I had been playing in the front yard. Hypervigilant about the unfolding drama, I became overwhelmed and forgot about her.

Tragedy struck. My father drove out of the driveway in a fit of anger and ran over and killed Suzy. Within minutes, he was out of his car, shaking his finger at me and yelling at the top of his lungs. Suzy was dead and it was all my fault. He blamed me. I was seven years old.

Shame button installed: I am worthless; I am not good enough; nothing less than perfection will do. To this day, I remember my father towering over me, and that feeling of dread, the terror and the shameful thoughts swirling around my head like a swarm of bees. "There must be something wrong with me. It's all my fault. *Everything is all my fault. I am not good enough.*" Immense sadness filled the place of joy that Suzy had filled.

On a deep subconscious level, besides the shame and lies I believed about myself that day, I also made a vow that would hide in the core of my being for decades: "I will never love anything or anyone like that again—ever." Walls began to build around my heart.

Children are amazing storytellers, but horrible historians. Negative self-perceptions are rarely true, but they can form the strongholds that bind a person to their pain, causing them to form beliefs and make decisions that can hinder relationships, past and present. The ego is an amazing and resilient part of every person; unfortunately, the defensive fortress it builds blocks the bad things and just as often shuts out the good as well.

Things did not get better at home. Alcoholism is a progressive disease, and my dad was getting sicker every day. My mom left him when I was eight. A short time later, he showed up at the house with a gun and threatened to kill himself if she didn't take him back. My mom convinced him to get help and called his father, who had him committed to an inpatient institution (probably an alcoholic asylum) for that day. He was 31 years old when he had a complete alcoholic breakdown.

We went to visit him. The image of that place still stands strong in my mind: the hospital-like setting, the sterile smell, the simple white room, my father lying depressed and defeated in one of the two twin beds. A gray-haired older man, dressed only in a diaper, shuffled aimlessly around the room. Today I'm confident this man was suffering from alcoholic wet brain: Korsakoff syndrome. Unknown to me, this would be the last time I would see my father for three years.

Divorced and Ashamed

The following day, on my ninth birthday, my mom packed her 1967 VW Bug and a moving van with all our belongings, and together we started the long drive from California to Washington State, where my grandmother had settled after marrying the younger man who had helped her destroy her first marriage. My mom was hopeful that the distance would deter my alcoholic father from visiting, and even more hopeful of forming a new relationship with my grandmother.

My mom returned to full-time work, and I was left with caregivers whose primary aim was money, not playing or connecting with me in any way. I entered a three-year period of silence from my father. My mind often ran through a series of questions. "Why didn't my dad call, or visit. What had I done?"

My imagination always came up with the same answers: I didn't matter, and I wasn't good enough. I grew to hate silence. My mom never said a word about him, and neither did I. Years later, I found out that a lawyer had warned her of saying anything negative about my father, for fear he would return and try to gain custody. But our silence bred shame.

Once we were settled in Washington, I started school, at the end of third grade. Divorce still carried a great stigma back in the 60s; I can remember feeling like I had a huge D plastered in the middle of my chest. I was "the divorced one."

It was during this time that I remember being taken to church for the first time, but it was just one more traumatic event. My mom left me in some type of classroom. It was test day. There was only one question: How do you spell the name of God? The answer was Jehovah, but I had no answer. In my magical mind, I failed. I failed to be a child of God; I was a *failure*. Arrow shot.

In addition to all of these, hold up the shield of faith to
stop the fiery arrows of the devil.

Eph. 6:16 (New Living Translation)

At that time, divorce was an unforgivable sin, and the church didn't help or encourage my mom as a new divorcee. Instead, they shamed and rejected her. We left and vowed never to return. The generational impact of that experience left me with an underlying belief that if we are rejected and judged by the church and its people, then that must be how God feels about us; therefore He, too, is rejecting. And rejection breeds rejection.

Today, of course, I know that God isn't the church. The church is made up of a body of messy, sinful believers and if our focus is on the sinful people, we'll miss God. I didn't know that in the 60s, but I sure do now.

The traits associated with being the child of an alcoholic were developing rapidly in my life: feelings of insecurity, worthlessness, rejection and immense aloneness. Fear of abandonment and rejection overwhelmed me daily. I believed that I didn't fit in or belong anywhere. I was convinced I was different, broken, and flawed. These feelings made up the fabric of my existence.

Comparison and jealously set in early. In my mind, everyone had a mom and a dad but me. Nothing was ever good enough, especially me. I had a shame-based, distorted view of self. In short, I was full of lies. The enemy was successful at his task. Arrows shot; my heart was pierced. The wall rose higher.

Sexual Abuse

When I turned 11, my grandmother separated from the younger man and moved in with us. Over a period of four years, during my visits, he had secretly sexually abused me a handful of times. I had learned my first sexual lesson from him at the age of seven: if you please a man, he will love you.

Love for me in these early years was simple; it meant being held, lap time and having 100 percent of his attention focused on me. I was so starved for attention and affection that his grooming felt confusingly comfortable. As I got older, he paid me to "never tell anyone." Secrets kept. In fact, for years I protected him and his dirty little secrets, as I felt and believed he was the only one who loved me. It was a sick lie.

Pedophiles are craftsmen of deceit. Sick as it was, it was *something,* and as many wounded and lonely hearts know, "Something is better than nothing!" From a very early age, I began to equate sexuality with love, but this deception leads down a path of destruction and near death.

My grandmother eventually divorced him, but the damage was done. I kept his secrets for many years. Shame is a powerful silencer.

Clinical Insights: What Is Trauma?

Due to enormous breakthroughs in the area of neuroscience, the most important fact today is that we can treat and heal trauma.

Some of the most noted professionals on this topic are Dr. Bessel van der Kolk, M.D., *The Body Keeps the Score*, Francine Shapiro, PhD, founder of Eye Movement Desensitization and Reprocessing (EMDR), author of *Getting Past your Past*, and Dr. Daniel J. Siegel, M.D., *Healing Trauma,* and Dr. E. James Wilder, PhD., co author of the following book noted, and his newest book, *Renovated.*

In the book, *Living from the Heart Jesus Gave You: The Essentials of Christian Living*, the authors emphasize that if we are to recover from trauma, we need to understand what type of trauma it is that we have suffered. They describe two types of trauma, A and B:

The absence of necessary good things—Type A Traumas:
1. Not being cherished and celebrated by one's parents simply by virtue of one's existence.
2. Not having the experience of being a delight.
3. Not having a parent take the time to understand who you are—encouraging you to share who you are, what you think, and what you feel.
4. Not receiving large amounts of nonsexual physical nurturing—laps to sit on, arms to hold, and a willingness to let you go when you have had enough.
5. Not receiving age-appropriate limits and having those limits enforced in ways that do not call your value into question.
6. Not being given adequate food, clothing, shelter, medical and dental care.
7. Not being taught how to do hard things—to problem-solve and to develop persistence.
8. Not being given opportunities to develop personal resources and talents.

Bad things that happen—Type B Traumas:
1. Physical abuse, including face slapping, hair pulling, shaking, punching, and tickling a child into hysteria.
2. Any spanking that becomes violent, leaving marks or bruises or emotional scars.
3. Sexual abuse including inappropriate touching, sexual kissing or hugging, intercourse, oral or anal sex, voyeurism, exhibitionism, or the sharing of the parent's sexual experiences with the child.
4. Verbal abuse or name-calling.
5. Abandonment by a parent.
6. Torture or satanic ritual abuse.
7. Witnessing someone else being abused.

(James G. Friesen, 2000-R, p. 75)

When a child grows up in a home where there's someone addicted to, for example, porn, sex, gambling, codependency, drugs or alcohol, and/or someone with physical, medical, or mental health issues, the focus is on the sick person and not on the child.

For the child, there's a lot of anxiety, fear, and chaos. It's like waiting for the other shoe to drop, or a sense of impending doom, or walking on eggshells, because the family system creates an insecure attachment. In the book I mentioned above, it's called *fear bonding* (James G. Friesen, 2000-R).

In the interview "Childhood Trauma Leads to Brains Wired for Fear," Dr. Bessel van der Kolk (author of the book The Body Keeps the Score: Brain, Mind, and Body in the Healing of Trauma) says:

> Children's brains are shaped by traumatic experiences, which can lead to problems with anger, addiction and even criminal activity in adulthood.

(Kolk, 2019)

When a child grows up with that type of anxiety and fear, they become hypervigilant and attempt to make their external world "ok" to calm and comfort their inner selves. They begin to live from the outside in.

For example, a child might grow up trying harder and harder to please the sick parent, but instead of comfort and praise, they're met with blame, shame, criticism, neglect, and abandonment. The cycle continues; the child reacts by trying even harder. There's a progression of fear, anxiety, and self-blame that develops into self-loathing and resentment. The whole family system becomes sick. Shame-based beliefs settle in.

When a child cannot calm down, they need connection
and comfort, not criticism and control.

(Jane Evans, 2019)

Some of the maladaptive responses to this kind of trauma and pain are caretaking, people-pleasing, addictive approval-seeking, perfectionism, performance, possessiveness, materialism, hoarding, intellectualizing, addictions, eating disorders, control issues … the list could go on and on. Let me also add flight, fight, freeze, or appease. These are all unhealthy reactions to pain.

Subconsciously, the family and/or society members put on a mask of denial to protect the diseased system. There's a deceptive underlying belief that says, "If they're ok, I'm ok." Their patterns of beliefs and behaviors (their *strongholds*) become a way of life. They live behind a mask of false identities and lose their true self—which is never developed because it is overshadowed by survival and defense mechanisms. This is a self-focused, self-reliant response to pain.

All types of traumas cause long-lasting damage. Most people when they think of the word trauma think of type B traumas which are also known as complex traumas. Some examples include armed conflict, posttraumatic stress disorder (PTSD), sexual abuse, terrorist attacks, school shootings, abduction, human trafficking, and the kinds of incidents described by the #MeToo movement.

We also need to be mindful of Vicarious or Secondary trauma which can be experienced when we witness a traumatic event. The trauma may not have happened directly to us, but the things we were exposed to can wound us. Even what we watch on TV can impact our souls. For example, our nation was vicariously traumatized by watching the hijacked planes crash into the Twin Towers on 9/11 during news coverage. For many people, traveling has been affected from that day until now, gravely and in multiple ways. Being careful of what we watch is imperative to self-care.

There's no fear in love, but perfect love casts out fear.

1 John 4:18

As a society, we don't speak much about type A trauma—attachment trauma. The unfinished business of our childhood includes the absence of security, significance, or positive regard. It can cause people to become so focused on things outside themselves for safety, approval, acceptance, love, value, worth, significance, nurture, validation, and comfort that they miss an authentic connection with each other. We become driven by accolades and awards.

In biblical terms, this behavior pattern is a turning to counterfeit idols and things of this world: finances, popularity, positions, property, status, or simply someone else to fill the void. The family may look amazing to the world's standards on the outside but inside the family system, there's a pervasive lack and loss of esteem, worth, self, or connection.

It's the belief that "something out there will make me happy and make me feel worthy." We get sidetracked pushing for greater gun control or better security standards—or higher levels of achievement or material gain—rather than looking at the real problem which is a heart problem, or better yet a "sin" problem. I'll talk more about the concept of sin and generational strongholds later.

We are creatures of comfort, so most people will repress or dissociate from their pain rather than face and feel it. It's a common experience to ignore events, stuffing them deep down inside the heart in the hope they'll never see the light of day. The trauma will become covered up with performance, addictions, busyness, avoidance, workaholism, etc., and the subconscious will store the pain for later.

Children especially do not have the capacity or maturity to process emotional pain or trauma. That is why these stored experiences begin to emerge or are triggered years later. Once again, time proves that it does not heal.

I've seen a lot of empty-nesters who, after years of being busy with children and their commitments at school, sports, etc., completely fall apart after the children leave home. All the unresolved stuff from their past pops up, as they are no longer able to contain the pain; many times, they're at a loss as to what to do.

To describe this unraveling and unpacking of our past trauma, I've created my theory, the *Jack-in-the-Box Theory*. We cruise through life unknowingly harboring old hurts and pain, dysfunctional beliefs and shame. We spend an incredible amount of energy subconsciously storing our secrets and silently suffering by staying busy and being preoccupied, driven or addicted. We are living from the outside in to seal and calm the horrors in our box.

We can be bouncing along, singing our happy little tune, when suddenly—like the straw that broke the camel's back—an event triggers our pain, the lid flies open and out jumps JACK: Junk that Adversely Compromises and Kills. JACK is the unresolved trauma, shame, and pain that harmfully hampers and destroys relationships. It kills joy, connection, health, prosperity, belonging, worth, esteem, and security. In other words, it compromises us.

When we build the capacity to face ourselves and our unresolved issues, they become gifts in disguise. It doesn't feel like it at the time, but if we can acknowledge that it was our own unresolved junk that got triggered, then we can begin to examine and resolve it. We can get free and heal. God and the world then stop being our enemies, and we begin to see that the real problems lie within ourselves.

As long as the problem exists outside ourselves, we stay stuck in blame and shame. But if we accept that the problem lies within, there's hope for healing—because the only thing we can change is ourselves. We begin to learn that triggers or strong emotional reactions that do not match our current circumstances are manifestations of our JACK.

Biblical Insights: Forgiving and Healing from Trauma

How we deal with triggers makes or breaks us and realizing this can be a turning point. Acknowledging and validating traumatic and painful experiences and the messages deposited on our soul is the beginning of healing. Sometimes the event itself isn't as painful as the lingering messages that created the shame-based self. We need to recognize, treat, and heal not only the trauma but the toxic shame messages and beliefs attached to our triggers.

This is God's love and invitation to heal: Are you willing? You do have the maturity to bear the weight of what has happened. Examine, look, and feel, and I, God, will help you.

Let me give you one example from my own life. Family gatherings usually become opportunities for me to examine triggers. One holiday, I was experiencing some criticism and blame from two family members, and I had an extremely strong emotional reaction. I felt angry and defensive. Then I became outwardly cynical, intolerant, and antagonistic—downright mean.

This behavior is completely objectionable to me today. It is in direct conflict with my spiritual ideals and life. It grieved the new me. This, in itself, was good news, because the old, hardened me would not have cared. I would have dug in my heels, stayed angry, justified my behavior, and then reinforced my wall to keep everyone out.

But the new me felt terrible about my behavior and attitudes. This was a healthy guilt. So I examined what was going on with me, and I asked God to show me the root of this pain. This is a holy pause.

As I started to write, the first thing I saw was my seven-year-old self cowering under my dad's shaking finger as he shouted his anger and blame over the puppy incident. Even though no one had been shaking their finger at me, the feelings were the same. Instantly I saw the connection that was being triggered. This awareness calmed my anger and compassion quickly filled the space.

Next, I asked God for healing and forgiveness, sitting at the cross, imagining His love and forgiveness pouring out. I went back to my family and confessed that the strong negative reactions I had towards them were wrong. I owned my emotions and behavior.

They did not make me angry; my anger was an old, unhealthy response to being blamed and criticized. Under the old family *don't talk, don't trust, don't feel* rules, I would have continued with my behavior and blamed it on everyone else.

Instead, as a family, we now talk, feel, and trust. The process for me included self-examination as I uncovered the true trigger and shared the experience and the feelings with my family. I offered gratitude through humility to work on my shortcomings that were offending them. I owned my JACK and the old trauma triggers which needed to be peeled away.

You ask, "Why would you ask God for forgiveness?"

It is so easy to say, "You made me angry!" But the truth is that my response towards any other human being today is my responsibility. The fact that I operated out of an old defense mechanism isn't God's will. His will is to love and be loved, and being defensive and angry isn't love. Love is sacrificial. It means confessing and dying to selfish desires and ambitions, dying to self, to desire His will and allow His love to flow through you.

If I stay stuck in anger, my channel to love is blocked. Part of healing my trauma is knowing that I no longer need to walk in anger as a form of self-protection. I can be free to walk in love and free from the bondage of the fortress I erected long before I knew a loving God was there to protect and help me all along the way. Now I trust His love and approval, not man's.

The truth is that, as I am right now, no one can ever hurt me again unless I allow it. There are no victims, only willing participants. This is an empowered, mature response to life on God's terms.

Owning and releasing my pain and old beliefs to God frees me to walk in love and truth. Humbly admitting and confessing when I am wrong and asking for forgiveness is all part of the practice that builds new pathways in the brain, empowering me to walk according to God's Spirit and His best-blessed plans for me.

Humility is seeking and doing the will of God. It is not thinking less of self, but being so preoccupied with God and His will that you are not focused on self at all. Humility allows God into the picture—His will, His emotions, His power—and eradicates the self-built fortress of pride, greed, lust, sloth, envy, anger, jealousy, gluttony, covetousness, fear, shame, blame, and/or addictions; in other words, *the power of sin.*

This is great news on two fronts. Firstly, on the spiritual front, God's love, truth, forgiveness, and power heals. One mistake believers make is thinking that spiritual warfare is just fighting a battle in the heavenly realms, but there is another battle going on right where our feet are planted. The biggest battle we will fight every day is the battle with our temptations, sins, and sinful nature.

Secondly, on the physical front, the brain can heal and create new connections—this is called *neuroplasticity*—healing trauma is possible. The process begins by uncovering, acknowledging, and putting words to what happened, then grieving or feeling the pain. Many people want to pole vault over their pain and just forgive, but it is so important in healing to feel and process the pain. Then we can begin to extend forgiveness. This is the process of letting go, even when it doesn't feel good. We can begin to allow God and His love to access our hearts.

Clinical Insights: What Are Adverse Childhood Experiences?

The term "adverse childhood experiences" (ACEs) was coined in the US in the 1990s by Felitti *et al.* (1998) who showed that ACEs appeared to be common and have a clear relationship with a wide range of illnesses and social problems.

Research has shown that Adverse childhood experiences (ACEs) impact health and increase the risks of various medical and mental health issues, including substance use disorders.

ACEs Key points

- Adverse childhood experiences (ACEs) are common and all clinical and medical professionals are likely to meet patients who have experienced them.

- ACEs can cause physiological damage to the nervous system and stress response mechanisms.
- ACEs appear to be linked with a wide range of health issues in adulthood, such as chronic lung disease, depression, and addiction.
- A trauma-informed approach to care isn't only important in terms of supporting adult survivors of ACEs but also to improve prevention and early intervention.
- Asking patients about ACEs and acknowledging their impact on health has been shown to be a helpful intervention.

Examples of Adverse Childhood Experiences:

- Sexual abuse;
- Physical abuse or neglect;
- Emotional abuse or neglect;
- Domestic violence;
- Substance misuse in the household;
- Mental illness in the household;
- Parental separation or divorce;
- Imprisonment of a household member.

Gilliver, C. (2018)

Tragically, trauma, drama, shame, and blame can all become normalized in dysfunctional family systems; this means that breaking down the wall of denial, justification, rationalization, or minimization can be a journey in itself.

Once the trauma is acknowledged, you can work towards resolving it. In the book *Living from the Heart Jesus Gave You,* the authors agree that type A trauma can heal well in a safe, mature, and nurturing community. In such a community, victims can begin learn to trust, share their needs and feelings, and then begin to feel safe.

Healing relational attachment is critical for the successful healing of trauma. Healthy relations and connections can restore hope, love, and joy. Research suggests that serotonin, a neurotransmitter associated with a sense of well-being, can be built in a healthy community. Building community and a sense of well-being are therefore vital for traumatized clients. Seeking help from a qualified trauma counselor or professional can also expedite the healing process. They are trained to build a therapeutic alliance and to treat trauma with evidence-based practices (practices that have been proven in clinical trials).

Some noted evidenced-based practices include: Eye Movement Desensitization and Reprocessing (EMDR), Emotionally Focused Therapy (EFT), Internal Family Systems (IFS), Cognitive and Behavioral Therapy (CBT), and Prolonged Exposure Therapy (PET). There are many others.

Many professionals now define trauma as a brain injury that can be healed, not a disorder. Traumatic events stick to the brain like Velcro. Neuroplasticity is the great news of our era; the brain can heal, and so can you!

The movie *Cracked Up* tells the story of actor and comedian Darrell Hammond and the impact ACEs had on his life; it is an attempt to break the silence and the stigma of mental health and addiction:

> My doctor said to me, "I don't want you to say mental illness, I want you to say mental injury." Let's tell the whole story. ... The worst crime isn't what happened, the worst crime is being expected not to talk.

(Hammond, 2020)

Hiding secrets fuels shame and typifies the wounded heart of the traumatized client. In essence, secrets keep us sick.

Clinical Insights: What Is Adult Children of Addicts (ACoA) Trauma Syndrome?

In 1939, the founders of *AA* described in their book, *Alcoholics Anonymous*:

> An illness of this sort—and we have come to believe it an illness—involves those about us in a way no other human sickness can ... It engulfs all whose lives touch the sufferers. It brings misunderstanding, fierce resentment, financial insecurity, disgusted friends and employers, warped lives of blameless children, sad wives and parents, anyone can increase the list.

(Alcoholics Anonymous World Services, Inc., 2001, p. 18)

In December 2012, *Counselor* magazine ran an article by Tian Dayton called *The ACoA Trauma Syndrome*. Dr. Dayton describes how childhood trauma impacts adult relationships:

> Studies on trauma, and more recently neurobiology and attachment, have more or less proven what we have long observed clinically, that the shocking, humiliating and debilitating experiences that accompany living with addiction do, in fact, literally shape our neural networks. And that the personality complications caused by the early pain and stress can and often do emerge years and years after the fact.
>
> This is what being an ACoA is all about—a posttraumatic stress reaction. Long after CoAs leave their alcoholic homes, they remain ensnared in repeating relationship patterns that are the direct result of having been traumatized in childhood. Old pain keeps remerging in new relationships. The names change, but the pain and relationship dynamics remain the same.

(Dayton, 2012, pp. 37–40)

..many traits are impacted by the family illness. For example: "hypervigilance, anxiety, and hyperactivity, always scanning for potential danger or repeated relationship insults and ruptures, and emotional constriction cause a desire to want to hide or shut down what we are experiencing on the inside, and unresolved grief".

ACoAs have suffered profound losses: loss of family members, disruption of family rhythms, and rituals, loss of a comfortable and reliable family unit to grow up in, and often the anxiety of wondering if parents are in the position to parent the child. ACoAs often need to mourn, not only what happened in their childhoods, but also what never got a chance to happen.

Traumatic Bonding, because it is so deeply disruptive to our sense of normalcy, trauma in relationships can impel people both to withdraw from a close connection and to seek it desperately.

Traumatic bonds are unhealthy bonding styles that tend to become created in families where there's significant fear.

Traumatic bonds have a tendency to repeat themselves; that is, we tend to repeat this type of bonding style in relationships thorough out our lives, often without our awareness.

(Dayton, 2012, pp. 37–40)

Traits of ACoAs

Many children of alcoholics or addicts develop similar characteristics and personality traits. In her 1983 landmark book, *Adult Children of Alcoholics*, the late Janet G. Woititz outlined 13 of them. She cited that ACoAs often:

1. Guess at what normal behavior is
2. Have difficulty following a project through from beginning to end
3. Lie when it would be just as easy to tell the truth
4. Judge themselves without mercy
5. Have difficulty having fun
6. Take themselves very seriously
7. Have difficulty with intimate relationships
8. Overreact to changes over which they have no control
9. Constantly seek approval and affirmation
10. Feel that they're different from other people
11. Are super responsible or super irresponsible
12. Are extremely loyal, even in the face of evidence that the loyalty is undeserved
13. Are impulsive—they tend to lock themselves into a course of action without giving serious consideration to alternative behaviors or possible consequences. This impulsivity leads to confusion, self-loathing, and loss of control over their environment. In addition, they spend an excessive amount of energy cleaning up the mess.

(Woititz J. G.)

These traits can also apply to children raised in dysfunctional families. If you're the child of an alcoholic or an addict, not everything on this list will necessarily apply to you, but at least some of it likely will.

ACoAs and relationships

Many ACoA and/or addicts lose themselves in their relationships with others. Sometimes they find themselves attracted to alcoholics/addicts or other compulsive personalities, such as workaholics who are emotionally unavailable.

> Adult children may also form relationships with others who need their help or need to be rescued, to the extent of neglecting their own needs. If they place the focus on the overwhelming needs of someone else, they don't have to look at their difficulties and shortcomings.

(Hinrichs J, 2011)

Often, ACoA will take on the characteristics of alcoholics, even though they've never picked up a drink. They will exhibit denial, poor coping skills, and poor problem-solving, and they will form dysfunctional relationships. Generational dysfunctional maladaptive patterns can be handed down with or without alcohol. This is the power of generational trauma.

Chapter Four: Addicted

Do not get drunk on wine, which leads to debauchery.
Instead, be filled with the Spirit.

Ephesians 5:18

Chemical Addiction

My chemical addiction started when I was 11 years old when I smoked my first cigarette and loved it. I hated the taste but loved the feeling; the thrill of scoring, the high of inhaling. Immediately, I started stealing and skipping school to smoke. I was addicted from the first puff.

At the age of 12, four of us girls sat down and guzzled a gallon of wine in 10 minutes. The effect was electric, the impact instant. I was hooked and couldn't wait to do it again. All my insecurities and fears vanished. I belonged! I was cool! I felt alive. It was like I'd been holding my breath my whole life, but now I could exhale. My new drinking behavior filled the well of unmet needs for significance, security, and acceptance. I lived to drink and drank to live; I was chemically addicted from the first drink.

By 14, I was smoking pot daily; by 16, I was using much harder drugs. I was kicked out of school multiple times and threatened with expulsion, but somehow always landed on my feet. Thus the overachiever and champion manipulator were born.

As I mentioned earlier, I lived a double life. On one hand, I was an above-average student, an athlete with the hope of a promising future. I was a jock, musician, and aspiring artist. But on the other hand, I was a stoner, a drunk, a drug addict, and a troublemaker.

In my magnifying mind, my life was amazing; from the outside, we lived in a beautiful waterfront home, I drove my own car, I skied every weekend, worked as a professional skier, and ran with a respectable crowd. But secretly, under the surface, I was a train wreck.

Behavioral Addictions: Approval Seeking, Codependency, Sexual Abuse, and Pornography

When I was 12, my mother remarried. My stepfather was a good man by the world's standards — hard-working, dedicated, caring— but had a glaring vice: pornography. Pornography was everywhere. There were pornographic images decoupaged on his end tables, lampshades, coffee table, and a large wall hanging; all of which moved into the basement of our new duplex, which was next to my new bedroom.

It saddens me today to think of all the people who believe porn doesn't hurt anyone because it hurt me terribly. It desensitized me towards sex and nudity and blinded me to the fact that nude pictures objectify women for men's pleasure and vice versa. It took what God intended for pleasure and made it perverse.

Porn played a significant role in molding my values. It caused me to believe that being sexual and being "good" sexually were some of the most important virtues for a young woman in our society. This attitude continues to run rampant even today. One friend recently reported that her single, handsome, and talented son told her he would marry the first woman who didn't want to have sex with him on their first date.

Years ago, while I was serving on the Sex Education curriculum committee for our local school board, I was one of the few adults promoting an abstinence-based curriculum. After one of our meetings, an enraged female student stomped up and yelled in my face, "Don't you realize what an abusive message you're carrying? Men expect us to have some experience when we get married or they won't keep us."

This mentality breaks my heart. This is a dangerous lie to believe. If women and/or men are only kept and valued in a relationship or marriage for sex, they are being objectified. Being used as an object of sexual pleasure is abuse. We can objectify people for other things as well, but sex is one of the most destructive and deadly. Lust breeds lust. It builds an appetite that if not tamed can lead to violence against our bodies, minds, and souls.

A mind possessed by porn will corrupt any healthy expectations of the marital bed. A couple interested in following God's design for sex will learn that it is intended for pleasure in a committed marital relationship. It was only after coming into recovery and learning about God's perfect plan for sex and relationships that I realized this truth.

Once I overheard a young man saying, "Men live by a secret creed: use the bad girls, marry the good." Religious people said, "Don't drink, don't smoke, don't chew, and don't go out with girls who do!" What? Who knew? Not me. From my experiences, the bad girls were good, and the good girls were bad.

My beliefs about self and what it meant to be a woman were disastrously messed up early. Most people have virtuous values and morals. In recovery circles, I would hear people share how they lost them when they drank or drugged. When I first got clean and sober, I didn't even know what value or a moral was. Now I see that from the beginning, I had a moral system that was reversed: good was bad, and bad was good. I didn't lose my morals; I never had them, or at least healthy or godly ones.

These lessons were confirmed by my biological father when I was 17. I hadn't seen him in years, but I often threatened my mom to go live with him during my tirades. Since the breakup from my boyfriend, there had been increasing tensions between my stepfather, my mom, and me. I'd become extremely angry and rebellious. One day I shouted, "Someday I'll go live with my father," and out of the blue, my mom surprisingly agreed.

I flew to Reno, Nevada, a pair of new skis in one hand and a ticket for the Freestyle Training Camp in Heavenly Valley in the other. I was in heaven. My dad's new wife—number three —smoked pot and he drank, so I got to do both. There was only one rule: make sure the car was in the driveway by five a.m. so they could get to work. The drinking, partying, gambling cities of Reno and Lake Tahoe were mine.

My dad was working on a huge commercial building project at the time, and I got an administrative job on site. With tons of construction workers, I had a date every night. Dad sat me down and told me about the birds and bees. These were his words: "Men have animalistic instincts that cannot be satisfied by one woman, so we need to have multiple partners." My dad had an open marriage; he and his wife were swingers. They would have sex with whoever, whenever—and that went for his daughter, too.

Subconscious and subtle, but seductive, beliefs formed for me at this age: people were objects to be used for sexual pleasure, approval, or material or financial gain. I was completely blinded by this belief, but it was safe to use people and not love them; love was way too painful. These beliefs led me to not only be abused but also become an abuser and a user of much more than chemicals.

I'm not proud of this confession, but that was the path I was on. This destructive, deceptive path led to the loss of many things: my health, real intimacy, true love—and almost my life. Only by

God's grace am I alive to talk about this period. I won't share details of the level of depravity my behavior reached, but suffice it to say there were many incidents which I honestly shouldn't be living to talk about now.

At the freestyle camp, we shacked up, smoked pot, water-skied, and trained on carpeted ramps. I was lost in a sea of pleasure-seeking, mind-numbing self-aggrandizement, all the while believing I was having the time of my life.

This was the era when, if you contracted a disease, a good doctor would prescribe the cure. Within a few years, though, this behavior could spell AIDS, which was untreatable and incurable in the beginning. It was a death sentence. But for me as a teen, there was no thought of danger or risk; I just wanted more, more, more.

Alcoholic? Addict? Me? Never!

After the camp, I returned to my dad's. One day while I was hanging out, I came across the book *Alcoholics Anonymous*. A handwritten note from my stepmom was lodged in the first few pages. It read, *"Dear Sirs, I believe my husband has a drinking problem. Could you please help me?"* One passage in the book caught my attention: *"Once an alcoholic, always an alcoholic."* (Alcoholics Anonymous World Services, Inc, 2001, p. 33)

I slammed the book shut, tossed it back on the shelf, and swore a quiet vow to myself: I would never be an alcoholic. I would never be like my dad. Then I promptly returned to my sick denial and ignored any signs of a problem. My life was surely normal in every regard.

Within a month, the insanity of my dad's alcoholism and violence escalated. My old friend, terror, returned and could no longer be chemically numbed. Desperately and thankfully, I returned to Washington. I never talked to anyone about what happened. I just slipped silently back into my shame and addictions.

At this stage of my life, I had no idea what addiction was. I didn't care. It would be years before I would learn the lethality of the illness I struggled with. What follows is some basic information that helped me to overcome my shame and have a greater understanding of the disease model and the moral model of my affliction.

Clinical Insights: What Is the Neuroscience of Addictions?

The addict's brain is abnormal. Trauma can play a part in changing the neurobiology of anyone's brain at any age and can increase the risk of becoming addicted, but trauma itself is not the cause of addiction. The truth is that no one knows exactly what causes one in ten people to become addicted to substances, or one in four heroin users to become dependent. Science still has not proven the "why" of substance use disorders—but it has discovered what happens in the brain of addicts that is different than normal social users.

There are extensive journal articles and books on this topic, so it's not my intent to do anything here but introduce you to the very basics of this science. But you need to understand, first of all, that the addicted brain is not the addict's fault. They became addicted because of a chemical response, like a cucumber becoming a pickle.

The cucumber has no control over the chemical transformation it goes through, but the result of that transformation is that it becomes a pickle. Once a cucumber becomes pickled, there's no way for it to go back to being a cucumber; it has to live the best life it can as a pickle. In the treatment field, we say, "It's *not* your fault you became addicted, but it is your responsibility to treat it."

Many people who subscribe to the moral model argue, "But didn't they choose to drink or use drugs? Aren't they just being stupid?" Yes—it's true that they did choose to pick up that first drink or drug. What they did not choose or realize was that, at some point in their using career, they would cross a line, where willpower alone would not be sufficient to help them overcome their cravings or obsessions. A chemical metamorphosis would cause an increase in tolerance, progressing eventually to dependency—these are symptoms of addiction.

If you believe in the moral model of addiction, you'll think an addict is just a stupid person making poor choices and needing to make better ones. That's partially true; they *are* making bad choices, but not because they're stupid. The disease model shows us the truth about the neuroscience of the brain. It helps us to understand that there's something much more powerful at work that hijacks willpower and/or choice and renders the addicted person out of their control. Let's look at the record.

1939: Alcoholics Anonymous

The book *Alcoholics Anonymous*, written in 1939 from the experiences of the first 100 persons who got sober in AA, stated:

> We are convinced to a man that alcoholics of our type are in the grip of a progressive illness. Over any considerable period, we get worse, never better.

(Alcoholics Anonymous World Services, Inc, 2001, p. 30)

What's interesting about 1939 is that it was a turning point in history for people struggling with addictions. It was the beginning of a movement that has grown into not just one society, but multiple societies of millions of people around the world who have recovered through the twelve-step model.

Besides AA for alcoholics, this is Narcotics Anonymous (NA) for opioid or drug addicts, Al-Anon Family Groups for family and friends of alcoholics, Codependency Anonymous, Cocaine Anonymous (CA), Adult Children of Addicts or Alcoholics (ACA), and Nar-Anon family groups for those who have families and/or friends with drug addiction—to name just a few.

Before the formation of this movement in 1939, alcoholics were diagnosed as hopeless and untreatable and considered incurable and disgraceful. Good doctors felt very little hope while treating them. One of the first female alcoholics who helped develop AA in Chicago, back in 1939, shares her story in *The Keys of the Kingdom*:

> Prior to this time, there was one doctor who had continued to struggle with me. He had tried everything from having me attend daily mass at six a.m. to performing the most menial labor for his charity patients. Why he bothered with me as long as he did I shall never know, for he knew there was no answer for me in medicine, and he, like all doctors of his day, had been taught that the alcoholic was incurable and should be ignored. Doctors were advised to attend patients who could be benefited by medicine. With the alcoholic, they could only give temporary relief and in the last stages not even that. It was a waste of the doctors' time and the patients' money. Nevertheless, there were a few doctors who saw alcoholism as a disease and felt that the alcoholic was a victim of something over which he had no control. They had a hunch that there must be an answer for these

apparently hopeless ones, somewhere. Fortunately for
me, my doctor was one of the enlightened.

(Alcoholics Anonymous World Services, Inc, 2001, pp. 270–271)

Dr. William Duncan Silkworth, one of AA's great medical benefactors, was also a proponent of the disease model. He had dedicated his life to serving alcoholics and drug addicts in a New York hospital for over 30 years when he wrote this letter to AA:

All these, and many others have one symptom in
common: they cannot start drinking without
developing the phenomenon of craving. This
phenomenon, as we have suggested, may be the
manifestation of an allergy which differentiates these
people, and sets them apart as a distinct entity. It has
never been, by any treatment with which we are
familiar, permanently eradicated. The only relief we
have to suggest is entire abstinence. This immediately
precipitates us into a seething cauldron of debate.
Much has been written pro and con, but among
physicians, the general opinion seems to be that most
chronic alcoholics are doomed.

(Alcoholics Anonymous World Services, Inc, 2001, p. xxx)

In 1939, Dr. Silkworth described alcoholism as a *"phenomenon of craving"* (phenomenon means "something unknown") and an *"allergy"* (an "abnormal chemical reaction"). So, at that time, medically, no one knew what was causing this abnormal chemical reaction.

1970s: Acetaldehyde and THIQ Builds and Creates Cravings

Fast forward to the 1970's, when much research was done on the relationship between alcohol consumption and opiate receptors in the brain.

In 1973, Drs. Pert and Snyder confirmed the presence of specific binding sites for opiates in the brains of animals (Schuckit, 1979). Two years later, Dr. Charles Lieber, chief of the liver disease and nutrition research program at the Bronx Veterans Administration Hospital, found that the same amount of alcohol seemed to produce very different blood acetaldehyde levels in alcoholics and nonalcoholics; much higher levels were reached in alcoholics. Dr. Lieber theorized that this unusual buildup of acetaldehyde was caused in part by a liver malfunction (Lieber, 1975).

At the time of Dr. Lieber's work, Dr. Virginia Davis was in the midst of a cancer research project in San Antonio, Texas. In her work, Dr. Davis removed brains for study from the cadavers of chronic alcoholics who had died on Skid Row. She confirmed the presence of large quantities of a chemical, tetrahydroisoquinoline (THIQ), in the brains of all the cadavers. After years of research, they discovered two things: firstly, that a teetotal rat injected with THIQ could be transformed into an alcoholic rat and secondly that, once present, THIQ could not be eradicated. A study on monkeys demonstrated no deterioration in the level of THIQ over seven years; once the buildup occurred, they had no way to reverse it (Ohlms, 1983).

Through additional study, Dr. Davis discovered a connection between the alcoholics' increased levels of acetaldehyde as noted by Dr. Lieber, the binding sites in the brain found by Drs. Pert and Snyder, and the THIQ she herself had discovered in the brains of chronic alcoholics. She realized that the acetaldehyde produced by liver dysfunction is dumped into the bloodstream and travels to the brain, where it is condensed with dopamine into THIQ. This process is repeated each time an alcoholic takes a drink; slowly but surely, addicts build up a cache of THIQ in the reward centers of their brain (Daniel V. Lane JD, 2006).

After extensive research on rats, it was proven that "depending on an individual's metabolism and other factors not yet fully understood, a human with this genetic liver dysfunction who drinks will eventually accumulate a sufficient quantity of THIQ in the brain to create an irresistible craving for alcohol. Once that level is achieved, environmental triggers will cause a craving for alcohol that cannot be ignored. The alcoholic then crosses over the shadowy line into a whole new way of life—a life in which he or she no longer has control over drinking. In AA terms, the alcoholic is then and will forever remain powerless over alcohol, and so long as he or she believes drinking can be controlled, the alcoholic will not stop" (Daniel V. Lane JD, 2006).

As addiction professionals, we see the immense potential for hereditary disease. Many professionals agree that if you have one family member with a history of addiction, the first-generation heir will have a 50 percent chance of being addicted. If there are multiple generations, add 30 to 40 percent for every generation. In my family line, addiction has been a destructive, deadly disease for at least four generations. Before my recovery, all my family members suffered and many died by its hand.

Today, when we look at the disease model, we can talk about observable symptoms. Every disease has a pathology, a path of symptoms. The symptoms of the disease of addiction include cravings, tolerance, reverse tolerance, obsessions, denial, and progression to dependency with withdrawal and post-acute withdrawal symptoms. It is an irreversible, chronic disease. Left untreated, it is fatal. Addiction is not curable—but it is treatable. This is great news for today's addicted population.

> Addiction is a primary, chronic disease of brain reward, motivation, memory, and related circuitry. Dysfunction in these circuits leads to characteristic biological, psychological, social and spiritual manifestations. This is reflected in an individual pathologically pursuing reward and/or relief by substance use and other behaviors.

> Addiction is characterized by the inability to consistently abstain, impairment in behavioral control, craving diminished recognition of significant problems with one's behaviors and interpersonal relationships and dysfunctional emotional response. Like other chronic diseases, addiction often involves cycles of relapse and remission. Without treatment or engagement in recovery activities, addiction is progressive and can result in disability or premature death.

(American Society of Addiction Medicine, 2019)

1990s: The Hijacked Brain

In the 1990s, scientists coined the term "hijacked brain" to describe what happens to the pleasure center or midbrain once it is activated by dopamine, a chemical neurotransmitter designed to help us survive and thrive. The release of dopamine can be activated by chemicals or behavior. Once the midbrain or "pleasure center" is activated by dopamine, it hijacks the person's frontal lobe.

We can now measure increases in dopamine levels based on the chemical or behavior acting as the stimulus. For example, our first kiss raises dopamine levels to 50 times normal, food up to 150 times normal, and sex can increase the level up to 200 times normal. These are normal chemical responses.

As stated, chemicals release dopamine. However, psychoactive substances, any substance recognized as a toxin or a poison to the brain, do more than release dopamine; they deactivate, damage, and shut down the frontal lobe. Interesting fact: according to Wikipedia, the world's most widely consumed psychoactive substance is caffeine (Wikipedia, 2020).

As the disease of addiction progresses, the frontal lobe (the part of the brain used for logic and reasoning) is severely damaged and shuts down. Therefore, the addicted brain's ability to reason that A + B = C isn't there. For example, if I use and drive (A), I could get pulled over (B) and I could end up in jail, with huge fines, away from my children or family—or, even worse, I could lose my children or family (C). The rational brain would make this logical journey, but in the addicted brain, such reasoning ability is completely gone, wiped out, turned off, and destroyed.

All decisions travel from the back to the front of the brain; but when the pleasure center is activated, those thought processes get hijacked in the midbrain, and never make it to the frontal lobe.

Unsurprisingly, drugs of abuse or dependence also increase dopamine levels. Alcohol, which is a third-class narcotic, causes increases up to 250 times normal. Benzodiazepines (our nation's silent crisis and new frontier waiting to emerge) and opioids (a subclass of narcotics) increase dopamine 350 times normal. Crack cocaine raises levels to 750 times normal and methamphetamine to 1300 times normal. Sugar is eight times more powerful than crack cocaine. Heroin, an illegal opioid made from morphine, is 50 times more powerful than morphine.

Behavioral addictions such as gambling, sex, porn use, video gaming, social media, and cell phones, all increase dopamine, too, and can hijack the pleasure center just as easily. I caution parents from allowing their young children to be entertained or preoccupied with cell phones or other electronic devices for any period of time. It's hijacking their brain and rewiring their pleasure center for more, more, more. Watch withdrawal symptoms kick in with removal. According to the New York Post the average person checks their phone once every 12 minutes, burying their heads in their phones 80 times a day. This is why we call it "Electronic Crack".

A healthy brain's response to these dopamine levels is, "Whoa, I've had enough!" But the abnormal response is, "Wow, I want more!" Substance use disorders are not about how much or how often you use, but *what happens to you when you use*. If you find yourself using more than you intended, or using when you swore you'd never do it again, then chances are you're suffering from the diseased brain—the abnormal response.

So why have substance use disorders become increasingly destructive and deadly during our Opioid Crisis? In the simplest terms, when you bought drugs off the streets back in the 1970s, you got what you bought. In today's street drug market, however, you have no idea what you're getting. One case in point: Prince took a pill he bought believing it was Vicodin, but it was a counterfeit tablet, containing fentanyl. It caused his overdose and death. Thousands of cases just like this one are happening all over the world.

Manufacturers in China and Mexico started making fentanyl, a narcotic that's 100 times more powerful than morphine, and carfentanil which is 100 times more powerful than Fentanyl, and

10,000 times more powerful than morphine. These substances are sold over the internet, with pill machines able to press these deadly chemicals into counterfeit pills that have resulted in thousands of overdoses and deaths.

I wish I could shout this message from the highest mountaintops around the world: when a person's disease has progressed into dependency and the hijacked brain is in control, they are not going to stop and think, "Where did this drug come from? What could it do to me? Are my children safe?" That would be reasoning from a healthy, rational brain. But an addict's diseased brain is shut off, driven not only by pleasure but also by its need to stop the pain of "dope sickness" or withdrawal.

These people aren't stupid, idiots, weaklings, or pieces of s—, but these are terms used by most of my clients to describe themselves. This is the deep-seated shame that debilitates their lives and fuels them to seek more relief. This is the stage where they end up doing shameful, regrettable things that can fuel another round of insanity—if they survive.

As addictions specialists, we are trained that once an addict crosses over into *reverse tolerance*, where the dopamine receptors start shutting down, creating greater cravings, it is only a matter of time before the client will overdose and possibly die.

These are human beings who have crossed over into a world of powerlessness and loss of control. They don't need to get smarter or try harder or get stronger. They need to seek help. They're individuals worthy of love and respect—and, most importantly, treatment.

Addicts who were once labeled hopeless and untreatable are now treatable. The disease is still not curable, but it is treatable. This is great news for our society. We can provide hope for the hopeless.

If you find yourself struggling with an addiction, please seek help today. Treatment centers, twelve-step programs, and professionals are available in every community. Seek help now. This is a progressive, chronic, fatal disease; unless you get help, it will kill you.

Reach out your hand for help today. You're worth it.

I wasn't broken. I was sick, and when you're sick you got to let the people who care about you help.

(Ventimiglia, *This Is Us*, 2019)

Chapter Five: Hitting Bottom

I will give you a new heart and put a new spirit in you; I will remove from you your heart of stone and give you a heart of flesh.

Ezekiel 36:26

Domestic Violence

Living in Colorado at 23 years old, I was drinking and drugging my way through the town's men, jobs, and homes when, finally, I landed the perfect man. He partied just like me. And we were off. Forget the dream of professional skiing; I was too drunk to get out of the bars, and now I had a full-time supply of my favorite drug, cocaine, so it was an all-night party every night. If you've seen the movie *Blow*, well, that was my reality.

Thanksgiving night 1983, my boyfriend and I, after spending the holiday drinking and drugging into the early hours, got into a rip-roaring drunken fight. Leaving him at the bar, I returned home alone, but all I did was sulk in self-pity and this drove me back to get him. I fiercely believed no one should be alone for the holidays—especially me! There he was, drunk and disorderly, ranting to his boss about all the raw deals life had given him.

With his boss's help, he was pushed begrudgingly out of the bar, which had long been closed. Fuming, he plopped into the passenger seat of my car, reeking of booze and stale cigarette smoke. He continued to rant, beating his fist on my dashboard ... until his hand slipped and broke the windshield. I slammed on the brakes in the middle of Main Street, furious. We both bolted impulsively out of the car. I felt a rush of adrenaline. My hand flew up and met his face.

As I turned my back on him, he rushed me from behind and forced me down to the ground with a violent shove. I landed face down (my first saving grace) into a deep pile of fresh snow (my second saving grace). He was swinging punch after punch; all I could hear was him cursing and screaming at me to give him my face.

The streets were abandoned, but multiple punches later, a stranger came miraculously out of nowhere, yanked my boyfriend off of me (my third saving grace), and then threatened to do to him what he was doing to me. Without question, he fled.

The stranger picked me up from the curb, a bloody mess, and escorted me a short distance down the cold empty street to the police department. An officer was assigned to my case; he loaded me into his squad car and drove me the 10 miles to the local medical center.

Memories of that ride and night still burn bright today. I have a white wool coat on. Blood is dripping down my face and nose. My mind is a swirl of shock, pain, and rage. The cop starts talking to me about some twelve-step program; a support group to help alcoholics achieve sobriety.

It turned out the guy who was now the town mayor had been the town drunk decades earlier and had gotten sober in the twelve-step program. He had equipped the entire police force with their message of hope for a hopeless condition. The cop suggested my boyfriend and I check out one of those meetings.

Shaken and disgusted, I thought, "Do you see a problem here? I didn't do this to myself. *He* has a problem." And right then and there I resolved to take my boyfriend to a twelve-step meeting.

The doctor expressed surprise as he noted nothing was broken. He reported my injuries were massive contusions and released me with my arm in a sling, two black eyes, and a referral to the domestic violence victims' assistance program. Full of pride and indignation, I retorted coldly, "I don't need their services. I'm fine."

Internally I thought, "My boyfriend better get it together, or he's out." On the other hand, my codependency caused me to believe what happened that night was entirely my fault. Deep-seated shaming and binding beliefs screamed in my subconscious, "There's something wrong with me, I'm not good enough, and anyway, something is better than nothing!" I had an attack of the "coulda, shoulda, wouldas" and "if onlys." This distorted and delusional thinking drove me right back into his arms.

It took a couple of days for me to find my boyfriend because he had gone into hiding. Shame does that. I knocked on the door. He opened it, took one look at my battered face and body, and broke down crying. He apologized over and over again and admitted he needed help.

Just as I'd promised myself, I took him to a twelve-step meeting ... but of course, I went only for him; I wasn't there for myself. He was the one with the problem, so back into denial I went. I was fine. At the meeting, my mind raced with accusations: "He'd better get this! He'd better do this! He'd better ..." I immediately took a job as a cocktail waitress because drinking at home wasn't going to fly. He had to stay sober. Not me!

About 30 days later, I came home and found him in a drunken rage. Interesting how patterns repeat themselves; this was like replaying my relationship with my father all over again. But I had sworn to myself I'd never be like one of the women my father had abused so violently.

Remember my stepmom in Reno? Well, years earlier, sometime after I had left, she had been found alongside the highway, beaten near death at the hands of my jealous father. I guess the open marriage thing wasn't working out for him. Yet here I was, in spite of my "never."

I called my local police friends. They came and escorted him away. Now that he was out of the picture, I was convinced my problem was solved, oblivious that the greatest problem of my life was still around: me and my dysfunctional belief system, my addictions, and all the unresolved pain and shame from my past. Denial is a powerful symptom of the addict's disease.

DUI and Incarceration

Within five months, I had lost a few more jobs and a few more relationships, and I ended up with two DUIs 10 days apart; those cops I'd called friends had turned on me. When I got handed the second DUI, I looked square at my arresting officer and snapped, "Don't you realize you are ruining my life! I just got one of these!" I chased that lie right into jail and into the hands of my attorney the following morning.

The attorney I'd hired the week before, after DUI number one, just happened to be upstairs in court that morning. With a little assistance from the jailer, I was released on a Personal Recognizance (PR) bond: you sign an agreement that you will personally appear in court—or else. I was too hungover to care what the "or else" was.

My new attorney drove me to pick up my vehicle which had been impounded half a county away and we stopped for breakfast en route. Curious, he questioned me. "You seem to be an intelligent, young, attractive woman—why are you doing this to yourself?"

Irritated, I snapped, "Are you kidding me? Those cops have got my car figured out. They're after the wrong criminal. They're just picking on me!" Today, I probably would use the word *profiling*, and I believed this 100 percent. They were the problem, not me. A sick denial possessed my vision.

He was adamant. "You're going in front of the toughest judge in the state of Colorado as a habitual offender for DUIs, and you're looking at a year in the state penitentiary."

Completely unaffected by this statement, I proclaimed, "Well, that's your problem. That's why I've hired you." I had no interest in staying clean and sober, only in beating this game and winning at any cost.

At this stage of my addictions, I was completely blinded by my denial and delusions. I was driven by the insane beliefs that I had a cop problem, a boyfriend problem, and a money problem. I honestly thought that once I got those things straightened out, I'd be ok. The truth was, regardless of those things, I was a bigger mess than ever.

Let me take a moment here to talk about the moral system of the addict. Part of the progressive nature of addiction is that the addict's moral compass becomes reversed: good is bad and bad is good. The bad is cool. It's a delusional power trip, but it's completely consuming. The progression isn't just about the chemical use but also about the shifting attitudes and values that become an antisocial morality.

The denial the addict suffers is shocking to everyone else because they can see the truth. But the addict is consumed by justifications, minimizations, and rationalizations, trapped in a complex bondage of deception. As their emotional state declines, the shame, blame, and rage get worse and worse. An elaborate excuse system blocks their ability to see the truth.

My attorney strongly recommended I go to those twelve-step meetings, implying that it would look good to the judge. Instantly I thought, "Look good? Oh, I can play that game. I'm all about looking good for the judge. No problem! I'm heading to meetings."

Looking Good to Beat the System

Returning to the twelve-step rooms, I had one desire: to please the judge. I had no interest in making any significant changes to my life. Amazingly, all these years later I still remember the second meeting like it was yesterday. There was a room full of men—and one woman. They were very warm and welcoming. They did not ask many questions; they just let me sit and listen.

They recounted tragic stories of alcoholic deaths over years past. Stories that will be forever fixed in my memory.

There was the woman who passed out in the snow and froze to death; her body was found after the spring thaw, having been buried by snowplows. A young man, who was found dead, passed out and asphyxiated in his vomit. Another man found early one morning, frozen to death, half in and half out of his car. He had passed out drunk the night before while returning home from a party and his family found his body early the next morning.

"Drunks die dirty little deaths," they said.

These stories were shocking, but my denial could not be penetrated. Minimization ruled my life: this would never happen to me. Back to the bar I went.

I played the system the entire time. I lied and pretended to be sober and clean to the judge. At sentencing, I was given one year in the state penitentiary; the judge then suspended 11 months and gave me 30 days in the county jail on work release.

My charade of lies continued. I would be impaired all week, and then show up on Friday nights for my jail time, playing the good behavior act, recovery literature in hand. After I'd completed nine weekends, my sentence was reduced and dropped.

During my jail time, my cellmate, who was also released Monday through Friday, got another DUI. She would listen intently to me extolling all the benefits of the twelve-step program; while we were both rejecting the program at that point, she ended up joining and got sober and clean ahead of me. God uses fools and drunks; He used me!

The Disease Model and My First Step

The disease of addiction renders the afflicted person powerless to control it, and that's why the first step of any twelve-step program is an admission of powerlessness. This isn't about admitting you are weak. It's about admitting there's something so strong that it commands your willpower and controls you and your choices.

The disease of addiction is so powerful that it takes the afflicted person to places they swore they'd never go, with people they swore they would never go with, and makes them do things they swore they would never do. They do not have choices—just obsessions, cravings and loss of control, complete and total unmanageability. In biblical terms: bondage.

Many people think the addict is weak willed, but the truth is the will is overtaken by a physical, biomedical disease. It overpowers their will and they have less power than is necessary to control their use. The disease is in control and they are left out of control.

A normal person, if they were to listen to the story of someone coming out of addictions, would be blown away every time by the endurance, resilience, and courage demonstrated during the addict in their suffering. Their soul-shattering stories of survival can leave the listener speechless. Recovering addicts are some of the strongest people I have been privileged to know.

Up to this point in my life, I'd always sworn I'd never drink or do drugs on the job, on the slopes, or in the morning. I'd never be pregnant and unmarried. I'd never have an abortion. I'd *never* be like my father. I'd never be a victim of domestic violence. I'd never be with a married man. I'd never be an addict or an alcoholic. I'd never be in jail.

In my last year of using—from May 1984 to May 1985—all my "nevers," and more, started to happen. My disease was now so powerful it controlled every action and decision of my life. I was powerless.

I'd been living with the cravings and obsessions controlling my life since the age of 11, when I'd smoked my first cigarette. The cravings took over immediately, and I kept using to overcome cravings. However, the cravings controlled me. This is the true nature of addiction; the disease renders you powerless and out of control. I was not stupid but sick. I did not need to get smart but was in desperate need of intervention, treatment, and help.

Thus I had two DUIs in 10 days, with no thought of the consequences. That's how powerful the disease of addiction is and how damaged my brain had become. Nowhere in my reasoning was there the idea that I needed to stop driving impaired. Instead, my diseased brain said, "Those cops have got my car figured out—I need to switch counties."

For 12 months, almost to the day, I had tried everything to control my drinking and drug use, but it landed me in a position of complete defeat and despair, full of shame, self-hatred, and secrecy; my false self was in full bloom. I, the great performer, player, perfectionist, and master controller was crashing.

Every defense mechanism I used to rely on stopped working. I was on a collision course with defeat and hopeless despair. I was losing the battle, or so I thought. In fact, I was about to learn just the opposite; these ingredients led to my surrender. It turns out they are prerequisites for vital spiritual experience.

Clinical Insights: What Is Shame?

Shame and guilt sometimes get confused, but the distinction is this: guilt is healthy shame. It is the awareness that we did something wrong. Shame, on the other hand, is toxic. It attacks the character; it says there's something wrong with us. In his book *Bradshaw on the Family*, John Bradshaw writes, "Shame is a wound" (Bradshaw, 1988).

Case in point: food writer and chef, Anthony Bourdain, committed suicide on June 8, 2018. He reportedly started his addiction on a family trip to France at the age of nine, where "watered down wine and cigarettes were allowed on Sundays." In later years, he shared that "I was an unhappy soul, with a huge heroin and then crack problem. I hurt, disappointed and offended many, many, many people and I regret a lot. It's a shame I have to live with" (Bourdain, 2017).

For the person growing up in an addicted environment, shame becomes not so much a feeling that is experienced in relation to an incident or situation, as is the case with guilt, but rather a basic attitude toward and about the self. "I am bad" as opposed to "I did something bad." Shame can be experienced as a lack of energy for life, an inability to accept love and caring on a consistent basis or a hesitancy to move into self-affirming roles. It may play out as impulsive decision-making, or an inability to make decisions at all.

(Dayton, 2012)

Anthony Bourdain was clean and sober at the time of his death, but my professional opinion is that he died as a result of his untreated shame. He believed a lie; he didn't have to live with his shame, because like addictions, shame is treatable. This is a message I want to shout from every rooftop in the world. Healing shame is possible.

Shame leaves us feeling unlovable and unworthy. After 16 years of research and two hundred thousand pieces of data, here's what we know. We are wired for love and belonging. We are wired to be connected. In the absence of connection and the absence of love and belonging there's always suffering. One experience in our family of origin can be translated as unlovable, which is the heart of shame.

Shame can be experienced from just one single event. The outcome of shame is violence, bullying, addiction, eating disorders, anger, porn, gambling, etc. Unspoken shame is incredibly dangerous. Most of us have two responses to shame: 1. Denial; I have no idea what you are talking about. 2. I know exactly what you're talking about, but I don't want to talk about it. Shame grows in the environment of judgment, secrecy, silence; these feed shame. But shame cannot grow in empathy. Empathy is a hostile environment for shame. Shame cannot survive empathetic connection.

(Brene Brown Phd., 2016)

Biblical Insights: Healing Shame, Physically and Spiritually

Empathy and sympathy which build compassion and connection are powerful healing ingredients for the shame-based survivor. There's a great movement now among professionals studying the neuroscience of compassion and how compassion heals the brain. Shame, like trauma, sticks to the brain like Velcro. Toxic shame left unhealed destroys lives.

There are three kinds of compassion: self-compassion, compassion from others and –greater than either of these—God's compassion for us. If God loves us and is compassionate towards us, especially us sinners, then who are we to judge or be contemptuous of ourselves or others? God doesn't hold anything against us, so why should we? Yet self-hatred, self-bashing, and critical self-talk are common traits for those entering into early recovery from trauma and/or addictions.

We need to learn how to practice new patterns to overcome the old. It's important to learn new brain skills, and so it's time to send the old, negative self on a long vacation. That part of us has spent enough time protecting us and finding maladaptive ways to avoid pain. It's all part of an old survival mechanism that is no longer working; it should no longer be allowed to work.

Instead, we can begin to practice allowing positive affirmations, positive self-talk, visualization, and self-compassion to come in. Our nature is to beat ourselves up for the wrongs we have done—but God has offered us forgiveness, approval, acceptance, and love. None of us is greater than God, so if He offers all these positive gifts to us, who are we to refuse?

*Therefore, there's now no condemnation for those who
are in Christ Jesus.*

Romans 8:1

"God-esteem" is more powerful than self-esteem. God esteems, values, and believes in us. If we can begin to believe and receive His love, we can start to see ourselves as He sees us: perfect, blameless, wonderful, and delightful! We can focus on and contemplate God's love. This is a powerful type of meditation that can bring healing to wounded parts of the self.

One way to practice this meditation is to find a quiet place and open God's word. In Greek, that would be the *logos*, the written word of God, His love letter to the world. Read through the book of Psalms and seek verses that describe God's character and love for you personally. In a journal, record each word that speaks to you. Focus, repeat, memorize, and practice saying these verses daily. This is the healing process of allowing God's word to fill those dry places.

Another Greek word that describes God speaking personally, instantly, and directly to our hearts or circumstances is called a *rhema* word. Rhema words have the power to transform the lies of the enemy in a moment. Let me give you one example from my own life.

Shortly after my grandfather passed away, my uncle dropped a bomb on my family heritage. He called one night and told me that my father was the bastard child of an affair my grandmother had. As a consequence, he went on to say, I was not really a member of the only family I had ever known. This was the first blow.

The second blow came when my great-aunt invited me down to her home to see pictures of my great-grandfather. What had seemed like a kind gesture turned into another arrow from the enemy: she wanted proof that I was part of the family and insisted I get a DNA test.

A great wave of rejection came over me. As I prayed and cried out to God, I heard Him say "Go to Isaiah 41." My tearful response was, "Where do I start? What verse?" Gently He replied, "Just start reading."

Through my tears I began to read and came upon these verses:

> I took you from the ends of the earth, from its farthest corners I called you. I said, "You are my servant"; I have chosen you and have not rejected you. So do not fear, for I am with you; do not be dismayed, for I am your God. I will strengthen you and help you; I will uphold you with my righteous right hand.

Isaiah 41:9–10

In a moment, I felt a wave of peace and approval sweep over me. Suddenly, I was seated in the arms of my loving Heavenly Father who knew exactly what I needed at that moment to heal my heart.

The enemy is a schemer and a liar, and one of his schemes is to get us focused on our sin and shame. He desires to distract us from standing on God's word, the truth. He works to destroy our faith in God who loves us. But God will help us focus on our true identity as His beloved, chosen, forgiven, a perfect masterpiece.

Practice inviting God to come into your hurts and pains. Trust Him to take the old and make you new, whole and complete. It is part of the journey of healing. Believe He loves you, because He does—and nothing is too big for Him to help you overcome.

Let me testify to this: that trusting God to tear down the walls I had built to survive was worth it. The fortress I had created was too powerful for me to tear down. But God handled the job; in my weakness was His strength. You too can let Him demonstrate His power. He is waiting to help. Invite Him in!

You are not alone. Build a community of safe people: a therapist, a sponsor, a support group, a mentor and/or friends. Find people who show you empathy and positive high regard despite your mistakes or failures. Identify the grace givers in your life, and shut out the fault finders—including that ruthless, negative part of self.

Remember, they win by making you believe you're alone. Good folk fight for us, when we show we need them.

(Abram's 2019)

People who extend grace, forgiveness, and compassion can help by modeling self-care and positive behaviors. Practicing mindfulness and other positive behaviors will begin to activate the frontal lobe and calm down those fight-or-flight responses. This activity builds the side of the brain that's needed to live a healthy, positive life.

Healing is not about getting smart —it's about getting well. It's about getting healthy. It's about getting rid of the shame and replacing it with love.

You cannot be comfortable in your own skin without your own approval.

Mark Twain

John Bradshaw, in his video on Overcoming Toxic Shame, shared some other simple tools for healing shame:

- Surrender—give up control.
- Socialization—be in a group or find one good friend to come out of hiding.
- Self-disclosure—start disclosing.
- Sensitivity—become sensitive to the family role you came out of and begin to do the opposite.
- Self-talk—get rid of the negative and begin to practice positive affirmations.
- Surface repressed memories and feelings.
- Self-love—begin to choose to love yourself.
- Spirituality—get in touch with your inner child and your inner life. Find quiet places. Get ok with them.

(Bradshaw, Overcoming Toxic Shame, 1990)

To strengthen positive pathways in the brain, you need to build appreciation and gratitude. Begin by practicing an ABC gratitude list. Go through the alphabet daily, naming something you can appreciate or be grateful for that starts with each letter. Building a habit of appreciation and thankfulness builds a healthy brain.

Whatever you do, do it! You're worth it. You may not feel like it in the beginning, but your feelings lie to you. Just because someone else could not value you, does not mean you don't have value. Your feelings of worthlessness do not mean you are worthless. They are just feelings, not facts.

Whether you feel God or not isn't important, because God is a fact, not a feeling. His word is true. The things He says about Himself and you are believable because He is a God of truth.

Value and worth are birthrights; God counted the hairs on your head while you were in the womb. You were born with worth, but something or someone stripped it away. Now is your time to reclaim it. You are worth it. You always have been and you always will be!

You are not what you do or what you have done! You are a child of the king, an heir to the throne. Put on your royal garment and crown, and stand secure in the sunlight of God's love and approval. Allow His Spirit to fill your soul with the truth; you are loved, forgiven, cleansed and righteous. This is your true identity. You are His beloved one.

> *The Lord appeared to us in the past saying: "I have loved you with an everlasting love; I have drawn you with unfailing kindness."*

Jeremiah 31:3

Why is this so hard to believe? What are the barriers that keep us from really accepting God's love? Besides shame, one of the greatest barriers is sin. Let's take a minute to examine exactly what that is.

Biblical Insights: What Is Sin?

> *So God created mankind in his own image, in the image of God he created them; male and female he created them. God blessed them … God saw **all** that he had made, and it was **very good** …*

Genesis 1:28–31

We, mankind, were made male and female. We were made in His image; the masculine and feminine each reflect His perfect workmanship. From the beginning, God's great desire was for a perfect relationship with His creation, to be one with Him. God saw *all* that he had made, and it was *very good*. This is our true identity.

We are God's kids, beloved and perfect as His image-bearers. We are the royal representatives of His kingdom.

In Chapter 2 of Genesis, the story continues. God creates and names Adam and commands him: "You are free to eat from any tree in the garden; but you must not eat from the tree of the knowledge of good and evil, for when you eat of it you will surely die" (Gen. 2:17).

In the next few verses, Eve is created and named. Then in Genesis 2:25, we discover that "the man and his wife were both naked, and they felt **no shame**."

So at the very beginning of time, according to God almighty, our Creator, we were very good, and we were unashamed! What happened?

In Genesis 3:1, the serpent, also known as Satan, a crafty creation of God's, starts to question what God had said, casting deception and doubt. He tempts Eve with the idea that if she eats the forbidden fruit, she will know as much as God (the sin of pride), and then visual pleasure (lust) lures her to take a bite. "When Eve saw that the fruit from the tree was good for food and pleasing to the eye, and also desirable for gaining wisdom, she took some and ate it" (Gen. 3:6).

Now, where's Adam when all this is happening? Right there with her. So what happened to God's command, "Do not eat"? Did Adam have selective listening? No; I think Adam was more interested in following Eve at that moment than in obeying God. The power of first loves revealed in Adam and Eve or maybe the first ever case of codependency? Putting the approval and desires of others ahead of God? Maybe … but back to the story. Regardless of the nature of his sin, he takes a bite.

This is a demonstration of the powerful destructive forces that wage war against man's flesh: persuasion, pride, perception, pleasure, and deception. At that moment, Adam and Eve bent to follow their desires despite the direct command from the Creator of the universe. That is sin. In Billy Graham's documentary, he said, "The world has one problem; that is sin." Sin is the original problem.

In the garden, we meet our three greatest adversaries. One: the world, with the power of its pleasures. Two: sin, a powerful force that dwells in our flesh and relentlessly opposes God at every chance. Three: Satan, who roams the earth seeking to deceive, devour and destroy.

What happens next? Shame, blame, and death enter the garden! Adam and Eve immediately attempt to cover their shame with a fig leaf and hide from God as he comes looking for them. Adam blames God for giving him the woman; Eve blames the serpent. Blame and shame go back to the very beginning of creation!

God has an antidote for sin, shame, and death. He says in Romans 5:20, "Where sin abounds, grace abounds even more." Grace (God's undeserved favor) and love are the great conquerors of sin and shame.

But it's not enough to know that God has a solution to our sin problem. We must also take responsibility for that problem ourselves. Sometimes our sin problem goes back generationally, so it pays to look back to move forward.

Clinical Insights: Looking Back to Move Forward

You may be asking, "Isn't this book about healing and getting past all this stuff? Why do I need to look back?" Maybe this analogy will help.

Living in Florida, hurricanes are a way of life. After almost every hurricane there is some form of damage. As Floridians we know the routine. Hire a contractor to evaluate the damage and submit a claim. We cannot start to rebuild before the evaluation. With that knowledge, contractors share their plans and costs for rebuilding. We too cannot develop a plan without knowing what needs repairs. How can we repair or rebuild our lives if we don't understand the extent of our damage?

One way to look back is a tool called a *genogram*. It is a way to examine the patterns handed down from one generation to another. The first time I experienced a genogram was in therapy back in 2003. I had been asked to interview family members a few weeks before my appointment. In the session, we started with a blank whiteboard and went back four generations. The patterns that emerged held great significance for my healing.

One of the most impactful was the story of my great-grandfather on my father's side, a traveling executive back in the early 1900s. During a trip to Colorado, he met an opera singer at the Leadville Opera House, and they conceived a child out of wedlock. That child was my grandfather, born in 1905. As an infant, he was abandoned by his parents to German immigrant farmers who raised him to work on their farms until he grew old enough to leave. The message left on the soul of an abandoned child is "worthless" and "not good enough."

My grandfather got married and threatened to kill his wife if she ever left him; he was terrified of abandonment and extremely controlling. Sometime after the birth of their first son—my uncle—my grandfather had an affair with his secretary. To get even my grandmother pretended to have an affair.

During this time, my father was conceived. My grandfather never believed my father was his son. He raised him physically, but abandoned him emotionally before he was born. On top of that wound, he spent his whole life in the shadow of his brother, the family hero. He would often hear the comparison, "Why can't you be more like your brother?" Shame filled his soul.

My father became the family scapegoat, the troublemaker … and an alcoholic. He would often say, "You'd all be better off without me." This is the kind of lie one believes when one feels worthlessness and hopeless despair. My father struggled with his disease and shame until his dying day.

Like my father and grandfather, I was abandoned before birth. I was conceived out of wedlock, and most of my life I had struggled with shame-based messages of "worthlessness" and "not good enough."

Three generations of illegitimacy, abandonment, and shame were uncovered that day, as we examined the genogram. It was the first time I saw the power and destructive forces of generational patterns and sins.

It's beneficial to look not only at behavior and belief patterns but also at emotional response patterns: avoiding, checking out, running away, cowering, acting out, procrastination, lying, jealousy, bitterness, comparing, blaming, complaining, judging, rage, anger, self-pity, defensiveness, anxiety, and fear—to mention just a few. These patterns need to be rooted out and dealt with.

Over the years, I have worked diligently to eradicate and heal my shame. Layers upon layers have been uncovered and discarded with the help of God, prayer, and the Bible, plus various professionals, support groups, family, friends, and lay leaders. Patterns run deep, especially generational ones.

Dysfunctional patterns and beliefs become so normalized that they become almost impossible to identify alone, so I encourage anyone on this journey to seek out community, lay, and professional support.

Biblical Insights: What Are Generational Sins and Strongholds?

He punishes the children and their children for the sin
of the fathers to the third and fourth generation.

Exodus 34:7

Punish in this verse does not mean what you think. "In Exodus 34:7, the Hebrew word for punish means 'tends to be repeated.' What happens in one generation often repeats itself in the next" (Scazzero P. &., 2017, p. 63).

So what are generational sins? They are unhealthy, maladaptive patterns of thoughts, behaviors, and feelings handed down generation after generation until someone begins to break the patterns.

> *You cannot change what you aren't aware of. We may be*
> *through with the past but the past may not be through*
> *with you.*

(Scazzero, 2017)

Looking back over generations can give us the wider awareness needed to change unhealthy and damaging patterns, which can bring deep healing. We also need to be aware that we have a spiritual battle to be overcome as well. This is where *strongholds* come in.

In her book *Shattering your Strongholds*, Liberty Savard describes strongholds as something that:

> actually enabled you to survive terrifying
> circumstances in your past that were out of your
> control. This is one of the reasons you trust them. But
> if they're still in place in your life, they're providing
> access for the enemy's assaults. They're also

protecting wrong attitudes, beliefs, and patterns of thought you have learned to trust more than you trust the truth … We build strongholds, we rely on them to protect us and we fight like crazy to keep them. Strongholds and what they protect often cross and overlap categories of wrong attitudes, patterns of thinking, beliefs, etc. … What is important is to tear them apart and take them down, whatever their name.

(Savard, 1992, p. 48)

Pastor Jimmy Evans, in his *Fight for your Mind* broadcast, also had some words about strongholds:

2 Cor. 10:3–5 Our minds are a battlefield of good and evil. We are fighting an invisible war. We are equipped for the battle. When we get saved, we have multiple strongholds in our minds. Everyone is born lost into a world that is corrupted. All of us have developed multiple mental strongholds, whether it's from our family, entertainment, or our thoughts. A stronghold is a fortress that the devil uses to protect his place to control our lives. Fear, jealousy, anger, depression lust, worry, whatever it is.

Bondage is a house of thoughts. Every single bondage is a thought issue. They're built in hard times. Jesus came to set us free to liberate us from the lies of the devil. These lies were developed through failure, disappointment, and rejection. These strongholds are built in the bad times. He wants to put these thoughts high in our minds to keep our focus off of God.

The minute we hear the truth, the battle begins. Just like Adam and Eve in the garden, surely God did not mean that. Immediately the argument begins. Satan has one purpose: for you not to know God. Satan wants to put one high thing into your mind that keeps you from focusing on something good. We need to bring every thought captive. Bring into captivity – by force, by the spear.

Our eyes, our ears, our mouth are gates to the enemy. We are the gatekeeper. Any thought you do not take captive will take you captive. To take every thought captive, we have to take out the spear against the thought. I will not let a thought come into my mind that isn't approved by God. If Jesus says it stays, it stays. If Jesus says it goes, it goes. Obedience is to listen to Christ.

(Evans, ND)

This is a spiritual battle. Dr. Neil T. Anderson, author of the books *Victory over the Darkness* and *The Bondage Breaker,* has always shared the importance of dealing with the spiritual realm first.

Let's look at fear, for example. The Bible says fear can be a spirit (2 Tim 1:7). It follows, therefore, that as a spirit, you can renounce it or reject it in the name of Jesus and it will flee. If fear continues to be a problem, then it is probably the result of an emotional or psychological pattern of thought that has built a groove in the brain; like a vinyl record, it will continue to play its tune until there is healing.

Also, having a therapist who uses evidence-based practices like EMDR can help open up new grooves and/or pathways in the brain to overcome the old patterns and messages.

Over the past 30 years, my husband and I have been intentional to create a new legacy for our children and grandchildren. We are carrying the message of generational healing and recovery. It is impossible to escape the pain and shame of this world, but today my prayer is that everyone finds hope and healing to overcome the old negative sin patterns of the current and previous generations and grow in love.

Prayer:

Father, please come! In the name of Jesus, I bind the enemy's schemes to destroy and deceive me and my family by following old patterns of thoughts, beliefs, and behaviors that have led us astray. Your word says you purchased me with your blood, and right now I stand in the power of your blood to cleanse me and bring me a new life.

Please allow your Spirit to help me overcome any old patterns that no longer serve you. I desire to live according to your word and your will. I ask that you release me from the bondage of old strongholds, and/or spirits, namely _____, so that I may be free to live and love again according to your Spirit and your word. Bind my mind to your truth and continue to give me the grace to renounce the old ways in me, that you might rise in power and help me and future generations overcome the old sin patterns and strongholds, one day at a time.

Help me not grow weary as we fight this battle together. You are my greatest stronghold and tower of strength. May I continue to lean into you and trust you completely with every part of my being. Thank you in advance that you are tearing down the old defenses and creating in me a new heart and a new Spirit that will stand as a mighty fortress in Christ to meet every need. Forgive me for attempting to manage my own life with my old ways, and accept my confession as a commitment to being surrendered to you, your will, your life, and your Spirit, under your loving hands. I need you and desire you above all. I love you! Eternally Yours!

The weapons we fight with are not the weapons of the world. On the contrary, they have divine power to demolish strongholds.

2 Corinthians 10:4

Chapter Six: Modern-Day Miracle

I love the Lord, for he heard my voice; he heard my cry for mercy. Because he turned his ear to me, I will call on him as long as I live. The cords of death entangled me, the anguish of the grave came over me; I was overcome by distress and sorrow. Then I called on the name of the Lord: "Lord, save me!" The Lord is gracious and righteous; our God is full of compassion. The Lord protects the unwary; when I was brought low, he saved me. Return to your rest, my soul, for the Lord has been good to you. For you, Lord, have delivered me from death, my eyes from tears, my feet from stumbling, that I may walk before the Lord in the land of the living.

Psalms 116:1–9

My Miracle

The night of my last drink, I had promised a friend I would meet her early the next morning for a very important management seminar. I insisted I was only going to stop at the bar for one drink. She argued her point ("You know what happens to you when you drink"), but I was adamant. "Not this time! Really! I'm just going to have one and go home." I meant it this time—just one!

The evening went like this: I had one drink, and that went so well I had another. Then I noticed the time and rationalized, "It's only eight o'clock; I could go until ten." At ten o'clock, I thought, "I could go until midnight." Then one of my drug dealer friends came into the room and the game was on. My frontal lobe shut down.

At 4:15 a.m., I passed out with an almost empty fifth sitting by my side and no thought of where I needed to be that morning. I had promised my ride we would depart at 6 a.m. When I came to, it was 6:15 a.m. Gripped with horror and disgust, I rushed home, only to discover a slew of messages berating my behavior and repeated *I told you so*'s on the answering machine. My ride was gone.

Despondently dragging myself upstairs, I passed out, muttering to myself and the universe that I didn't want to wake up from this one.

When I came to, a few hours later, something in me had changed. I knew what those people in the twelve-step rooms had said was true: I was an alcoholic and an addict. I had lost the ability to control my use. I needed help. I needed God, those steps, and those people.

At that moment, I needed and wanted what they had. I had heard stories of people who in their hour of desperation got on their knees, sought a God they did not believe in, and had an experience. This was my moment.

Getting on my knees with all the honesty, sincerity, and humility of a dying person, I said a very simple prayer. "God, I don't know who you are, where you are or what you are, but if you are, I can't live like this another day."

Instantly, I felt a presence flood my being from my head to my toes and a voice that audibly and gently spoke my name, "Laura. You will never have to feel this way again. You will never have to live this way again." And I felt a physical lifting of the obsession, compulsion, and desire to drink and drug. The problem was removed. I did not quit; I was freed.

Free! Free from the need to use any mood-altering chemical. This was a miracle; every morning that past year I'd been controlled by the obsessions and cravings to use. I had been lost in a sea of despair and hopelessness. But now that the cloud was lifted, I could see the truth.

In my moment of desperation, He faithfully revealed His power and love for me. God released me from the bondage of my disease and freed me from the compulsions and desires that had held me captive for so many years.

Some people might think this was the greatest miracle, but I think the greater miracle was being given the ability to see my needs and let someone in to help. Being released for one moment to be willing to seek a God I did not know or believe in, who suddenly and miraculously became real, alive, and personal, was indeed a real miracle.

Even after all these years clean and sober, I vividly remember the experience and feelings of that morning, May 3, 1985. One day at a time, I trust God to keep me free from the obsession, compulsion, and desire to use any mood-altering chemicals. I give Him all the credit for being clean and sober. In my surrender and seeking, He does the heavy lifting.

He revealed His power that morning, but it took years to build the faith that today has become indestructible. Let's start, as I did, with some basics.

Biblical Insights: Who Is God?

This topic is as expansive as the multiple universes He created and is out of the scope of this book, but here are some biblical basics.

In the beginning, God is described as the Creator: "Then God said, 'Let *us* make man in *our* image, in *our likeness*'" (Gen. 1:26).

In this verse, we see all three of the persons who make up the Holy Trinity: God the Father, God the Son (Jesus), and God the Holy Spirit. Just as water can manifest in three forms— steam, liquid water, and solid ice—God also presents as three persons, living, active, powerful, present, pursuing, and purposeful in our world and our lives.

God's many names also describe His character: who He is, not just what He can do. Some of those names and their meanings are Jehovah-Jireh (the Lord will provide), Jehovah-Rapha (the Lord will heal), Jehovah-Shalom (the Lord our peace), Jehovah-Tsidkenu (the Lord our righteousness). His names reveal His nature and describe who He is.

What's even more awesome news is that He doesn't only give us provision, healing, peace, or righteousness; He gives us Himself. He deposits His life into us so we are filled with His power, gifts, and nature. *Incarnational reality* is a term coined by Leanne Payne, from Pastoral Care Ministries, Wheaton, IL, meaning "collaboration with the Holy Spirit within us as God reclaims and restores us to our original created selves." The great evangelist Major Ian Thomas called it the *exchanged life*; our nature, our heart, our will, and our lives are exchanged with His. The old nature, life, and heart are gone, and the new has come.

> *Therefore, if anyone is in Christ, he is a new creation.*
> *The old has passed away; behold, the new has come.*

2 Corinthians 5:17 (ESV)

One of God's greatest characteristics is his unconditional love. In Exodus 34:5–6 (NLT), "The Lord passed in front of Moses, calling out, 'Yahweh, The Lord! The God of compassion and mercy! I am slow to anger and filled with unfailing love and faithfulness.'"

In 1 John 4:16b, we hear that "God is love. Whoever lives in love lives in God, and God in him." Simply put, God is love and truth. So what are the characteristics of this type of unfailing love?

Biblical Insights: What Is Unfailing Love?

Years ago, Pastor Charles Swindoll captured my attention with the ABCs of love: "I **accept** you as you are. I **believe** you are valuable. I **care** when you hurt."

The Greek language describes different types of love. Here are four:

- *Eros*: sexual desire

- *Phelia*: brotherly love, deep friendship

- *Storge*: a family bond

- *Agape*: love by choice and act of the will

Agape love only seeks your highest good. It is an undefeatable goodwill that, unlike the other types of love, is not dependent on chemistry or a feeling; this love is dependent on a decision. That's the type of love God has for you. He is the most dependable personality in the universe. His love is constant and does not go up and down based on feelings. He is love— therefore, He loves you!

In 2 Samuel 9, we read the story of King David desiring to show God's kindness to anyone still left of Saul's household. His request brings him to Mephibosheth, Jonathan's son, who had been crippled at five, when his nanny fell while running to hide him after his father and grandfather were killed. To further camouflage his true identity as heir to the throne, his name was changed to mean "despised or shamed one."

Besides being crippled in hiding, Mephibosheth is ashamed, abandoned, and orphaned out of fear, because typically once a ruler takes his rightful place as king, he will set out to kill every enemy to his throne. But not King David; he seeks out his enemy's grandson to bless him with the kindnesses of God, having made a covenant with his father, Jonathan, 25 years earlier—a covenant of love.

Pastor Rich Lively, the Lead Pastor of First Baptist Church of Cocoa, Florida, was kind enough to share his sermon notes from his study of God's love and kindness described in the Hebrew language, he writes this:

> This word comes from the Hebrew word "hesed," which is described as a "tenacious love and dedication with no end that will not give up or let go regardless of circumstance." In shorthand, it is "enduring eternal undeserved love and mercy!" The original root of it means "eagerness or keenness to act" so in this context we see a king eager to show love and kindness to someone even though it was not deserved.

This type of love and kindness is called grace.

This picture of God's grace is also called a foreshadowing of Christ; Christ, the King of Kings and Lord of Lords, does not seek to destroy us but seeks us eagerly to bestow on us His love and dedication with no end, regardless of our circumstance; to give us His enduring, eternal, undeserved love and mercy.

Remember the story of Adam and Eve hiding in their blame and shame? God was seeking them out. He never gave up on them; in fact, He pursued them. This is an awesome demonstration of his love. But wait, there's more!

In Genesis 3:14-20, God lays out to Adam and Eve the natural consequences for their sin. (Yes, sin carries natural consequences.) Some would say this was God punishing his children, but what I see is a loving God laying a foundation for his children to understand the boundaries between trusting God and obedience versus trusting self, pride, which in turn produces rebellion. Pride came before the fall and fueled the act of rebellion which led to our fall from grace. These are the natural consequences of deadly sins.

But God, in spite of the sins of Adam and Eve, granted his fallen creation an amazing gift which follows in Genesis 3:21. "The Lord God made garments of skin for Adam and his wife and clothed them." He clothed them using animal skin; a blood sacrifice was made to *cover the sin and shame* of Adam and Eve.

This was another foreshadowing of Christ, the Son of God, who lived to die on a cross, shedding His blood for the sins of the world. From the beginning, God had a better plan to help us overcome death, sin, and shame: the sacrifice of Himself through His Son, Jesus, on the cross for our sins.

The Bible is clear. In Romans 3:23, "All have sinned and fall short of the glory of God," but in Romans 6:23 we see "For the wages of sin is death, but the **free gift** of God is eternal life in Christ Jesus our Lord." The wage is death, and a price has to be paid.

What I don't understand is why anyone would work so hard to be good to pay a wage that God has already paid. All we have to do is accept the free gift of God; the debt has been paid, canceled. Christ, the free and sacrificial gift of God, laid down His life for us all and takes away the sins of the world—our sins. What an amazing payment plan and what amazing love!

This is the greatest demonstration of love ever. It's all-inclusive and free. God's loving desire is that none should perish. God is on the pursuit, promising life and love, eternally and abundantly.

> *But God demonstrates his own love for us in this; while we were still sinners, Christ died for us.*

Romans 5:8

Most religions preach and believe that if you do this or do that for God, then God will …, and then you will … But true biblical Christianity is the only religion in the world that says this: God did it for you so you don't have to! He loves us and He knew from the beginning that healing or saving ourselves would be too great a task for us. There's only one Savior, and we are not it. This is great news! We are free from the responsibility of saving ourselves, our families, and our world. We have a loving God who wants to do it for us.

God does not want us to hide our pain and shame, and He especially doesn't want us stuck in blame. Counterfeit cures don't heal our hurts; they only make them worse. Secrets keep us sick. Turn to Him! He desires to fill every broken place in you with His love, forgiveness, and joy. Give Him a chance! What do you have to lose?

There's a promise in Exodus 34:7b (NLT):

I lavish unfailing love to a thousand generations. I forgive iniquity, rebellion, and sin. But I do not excuse the guilty. I lay the sins of the parents upon their children and grandchildren; the entire family is affected – —even children in the third and fourth generations.

We once were guilty, but now we're not. When Christ died on the cross, His blood not only covered our sins but cleansed them as well. He cleansed us from all unrighteousness. In other words, He made us right with God. He bridged the gap between the human and the holy.

He made a way for us to live in the presence of a perfect God as perfect human beings. Not because of what we have done, but because of what He has done. We've been stamped and sealed with his approval and love—so when God looks at us through the blood of Christ, He sees us as blameless and spotless children of God. We are perfect in His eyes. This is our true identity. Self-esteem is limiting, but God's esteem is without end!

Let's talk more about our true selves and our false selves.

Biblical Insights: Who Am I? False Self vs True Self

When we pour our identity into what we "do," it becomes part of our false self. Brennan Manning, author of *Ruthless Trust: The Ragamuffin's Path to God*, calls it *the imposter*. This is the child who has erected a wall, a fortress, to protect anyone seeing the shame-based core self; it is a cover-up, developed from a web of self-protective lies. (Manning, 2000)

> *Every man carries a wound ... And every wound, whether it's assaultive or passive, delivers with it a message. The message feels final and true, absolutely true, because it is delivered with such force. Our reaction to it shapes our personality in very significant ways. From that flows the false self.*

(Eldridge, 2001, p. 72)

John Eldridge's theory is that our enemy, the devil—described in the Bible as the father of lies—has been shooting arrows into our hearts and spends every day attempting to pull us back into the wounds.

Even after a radical deliverance and becoming a Christian, Eldridge writes, "The wounds remained ... My arrows were still lodged deep and refused to allow some angry wounds inside to heal" (Eldridge, 2001).

This was my story, the story of my father, and my father's father. The wounds of abandonment and fatherlessness shot the

arrows of *worthless, forgotten, don't matter, and not good enough.*
Generational patterns of fierce independence and self-reliance
prevailed, and strongholds and beliefs followed: don't need, don't
trust, don't feel; keep secrets, suffer in silence, stay in control, admit
no one. The end result: the heart is locked in shame, and self-erected
walls are cemented in place to guard against rejection and pain.

Developmentally, all of us are born asking important
questions. Am I worthy? Do you love me? Am I valuable? Do I
belong? Am I safe? These are what we call core needs—needs for
love, approval, acceptance, nurture, value, worth, significance,
security, and belonging. If these needs go unmet, we begin to turn
outside of ourselves. This is attachment trauma. We attempt to
compensate by turning to the world for connection and answers,
seeking acceptance, love, approval, and belonging.

Unfortunately, we live in a fallen and unaffirmed world.
Many people have experienced more rejection than acceptance. Yet
we try harder to get what we need, until we give up and collapse,
concluding we are nothing. The problem is that we are allowing the
world to define who we are. If someone doesn't like us, we're not
likable; if someone isn't there for us, we believe we're not worthy.
Arrows shot.

So we try to pump up the broken, shame-based self with the
false self by using pleasure, performance, perfectionism,
philanthropy, prestige, positions, property, and people—things of the
material world which yield dead fruit. This strategy might work
temporarily, but eventually, we will have to face feeling empty,
alone, disconnected, and worthless. Those things are all counterfeits.

In an attempt to pump itself up, our ego works to boost our
self-esteem. When we use outward actions to feel worthy, we are
using performance to build our self-esteem. EGO stands for edging

God out. It is a self-reliant activity to build self-esteem by "doing" instead of "being".

The problem is that we are born with a God-shaped hole, and God's love is the only remedy. When we replace Him with things of this world, we are worshipping idols. Idols don't heal. They don't change or transform hearts and lives; they don't love us back. We use them and they use us.

The ultimate sin of our society is using, putting things of this world ahead of God. We use other people, sports, stuff, money, work, and pretty much anything else we can to feel good about ourselves. We are consumers, objectifying and projecting our unmet needs for worth and belonging onto whatever or whoever is closest.

Breaking this pattern and shedding our false self is like breaking an addiction. Many times, we become dependent on the very behaviors we're using to prop up our ego and esteem: social media, caretaking, busyness, rescuing, chemical and behavioral addictions.

Roles can be addictive, as well; we can find our self-esteem in being a parent, volunteering, or even climbing the ladder of success with a prestigious position. After the kids move away, the job or commitment ends, we begin to look for something else to "do" to feel better about ourselves. Sometimes losing these roles can feel like death to our identity; there may even be a grief process in letting go to accept our true identity.

Our perfect identity is rooted in who God says we are, not in what we "do". His perfect love fills and completes us. He created us to be relational first with Him, then with others. We belong to Him. We are His children (John 1:12), his friend (John 15:5), beloved (Deut. 33:12), forgiven (1 John 1:9), chosen (John 15:16) ... the list goes on and on.

God don't make no junk! We are children of the King, heirs to His throne. We can put on our royal garments every morning and walk in His love and approval every day. No one can ever steal this from us. It is our true identity, our true self. We are not what we "do" or what awards we achieve or how much money we possess or what positions we hold. We are royalty because of whose we are. This true identity can never be taken away. We can rest in "being" His.

I have been crucified with Christ and I no longer live, but Christ lives in me. The life I now live in the body, I live by faith in the Son of God, who loved me and gave Himself for me.

Galatians 2:30

Chapter Seven: Journey of Transformative Healing and Recovery

I call heaven and earth to witness against you today,
that I have set before you life and death, blessing and
curse. Therefore choose life, that you and your
offspring may live.

Deuteronomy 30:19 (ESV)

Bound by Shame

Even though the chemical obsession had been lifted, I had a new obsession: me. I was still bound by shame and regret, remorse and self-hatred. I returned to work, shame dripping from my pores; I was unable to look myself in the mirror, let alone anyone else in the eye.

My boss picked me up and gave me the standard lecture: when you're sober, you're a decent, loyal, and hard worker, but when you drink (drugging was my secret), something happens to you. She described the personality change that took me from being one of her best employees to being an unreliable, despairing wreck.

Back to meetings I went, with a new willingness to do whatever was asked of me. I'd come to believe that God was indeed alive; that was a great start, but it was only the beginning of a journey of healing that would span my lifetime—and, I believe, the generations to come. Subconsciously I was still captivated and driven by distrust, shame, and blame. God wanted to turn them into victory, purpose, and destiny.

The members of the group strongly suggested that women stick with women, but I found it a struggle to stay away from men.

My worth was still tied to the lie that I had to have a man in my life to be someone. On one hand, I thought I needed a man to be valuable—but on the other, many years earlier I had vowed I'd never love anyone or anything again. My heart was like a sealed vault: locked up, unavailable, and impenetrable. A decision had been made. No one was getting in here.

Meetings and fellowship became my new home and family. My sponsor—someone who had been there, done that, who offered a solution and showed the way—convinced me that God had a message for me at every meeting. If I missed a meeting, I'd miss His message.

I had a new attitude towards this new way of life. I looked forward to the honesty, transparency, and vulnerability members displayed while they were sharing. I began to feel connected like I had found my people. The stories they shared validated my own experiences with my disease and in my relationships. For the first time in my life, I wasn't alone.

I now felt unconditional acceptance and love after years of feeling isolated in my shame. I'd walk away from every meeting with a feeling that God was speaking to me. And thus, I became a true listener. My new community accepted me just the way I was and promised to love me until I could love myself. More importantly, they said they'd love me until I learned to love others.

Bitterness and Resentment: Barriers to Love

After a couple of months clean and sober, I started spewing my bitterness about my father like a fire hydrant. A few months earlier, my DUI instructor had challenged me to forgive him. That suggestion triggered an enraged, explosive response: "NEVER!"

Now sober, I found myself reliving the resentment and regurgitating every painful complaint I held against him. "He never did anything for me! He never sent me a card, a gift, never made a call!"

In the middle of my rant, I heard a voice. "You're 25 years old. When did you ever send a gift, mail a card, or make a call?" The message stopped me in my tracks. A great conviction and humility washed over me like a waterfall.

I had not seen my father since my visit to Reno at 17. The last time he'd called was during my college graduation celebration, and the first thing I heard him say was, "Have you seen my parents?" Feeling the punch of rejection as he made no mention of my accomplishment, I'd snapped, "If you can't call to talk to me, don't call!" Disgusted and enraged, I slammed the receiver down. I hated him.

Now I was compelled to act by the voice I've come to know and trust as God's. I went to the phone; after three long-distance calls, I found my father in a substance abuse treatment program in Topeka, Kansas. He pleaded with me to come and visit. He shared that he had been thinking of leaving but my call had changed his mind.

To my surprise, the following statement came out of my mouth: "Dad, I don't have any money. I've just gotten a new job, and I'm only making $3.35 per hour. I don't have a driver's license. I don't have any savings. I'm not sure how I would do it, but we'll see." And then I hung up.

I'm in Colorado, and he's in Kansas. What do we do when we are met with a dilemma? We go to a meeting. And at this particular meeting, there just happened to be two people visiting from Great Bend, Kansas, not far from my father. The woman shared how her mother had just passed away in Great Bend and that she would be traveling there to settle her estate. She invited me to ride along. The man then told me that if I got to Great Bend, I could call him and he would take me to the treatment center in Topeka. He knew exactly where it was because he reportedly frequented it every Friday. Coincidences are God's way of staying anonymous. Today, I call them *divine appointments.*

I went to work that afternoon and my new boss asked me to take the rest of the week off because she couldn't afford to pay me. It seemed I was going to Kansas.

After we arrived in Great Bend, I contacted my new friend. We landed in that treatment center on the one day of the month that was Family Day for my father. I was the only family that showed up. We asked him if he'd like to attend a twelve-step meeting over lunch, and he agreed. He sat across the table from me, and during the opening of the meeting, he shared his name and introduced himself as an alcoholic.

A sudden shift happened in my feelings about my father. Having learned the facts about my own disease, what I now knew about being an alcoholic was that he was truly powerless; the chemical had taken control of his life like it had mine. He had been in bondage to alcohol. Addiction was his master.

At that moment, I felt a great weight lifting. My resentments were exchanged with compassion, love, and forgiveness. Freedom was granted to me that day. Peace and acceptance filled the space that had been inhabited for so many years by hatred and bitterness.

I wish I could tell you that from that day forward, my father and I lived a life of love and harmony. Unfortunately, I was the only one set free that day; my father, driven by his untreated disease, destroyed two more marriages, two more biological children, and his own life. He was found bleeding out of every orifice of his body in April 2001, having previously been guaranteed certain death from a bleeding ulcer if he ever drank again. The following month, he was found collapsed in his home having died a dirty little death.

In the same week I buried my father as a result of his untreated addiction, I celebrated my own 16 years of recovery. It was a very bittersweet month. The disease that killed him was the same disease that led me to surrender and receive a life I could have never imagined. My future was full of promises, healing, and hope. His was over. The disease had won and left a path of destruction, despair, and death in its wake.

In the past, I had sworn I'd never be like my father, yet for the longest time my life was a reflection of his. But now I was on new ground and a new footing with a Heavenly Father who was helping me become a better reflection of Him.

Clinical Insights: What Are Resentments?

I have a theory that our feelings are a battleground between Positive Mental Energy (PME) and Negative Mental Energy (NME; our ENEMY). Feelings are not good or bad or right or wrong; they just *are*. Emotions are energy in motion. This energy can be harnessed and used either positively or negatively, and what we do with it can either be healthy or not.

Anger, for example, is a feeling. It is neither good nor bad. On the positive side, it can help us understand when our boundaries or values have been compromised. It is a warning emotion that helps us identify when we feel walked on or violated. It is the energy that propels us to say "no" or "stop." A healthy response to anger is acknowledging that this is an emotion we need to listen to. It is important to examine and resolve it by setting boundaries and asking for what we need or want, without playing victim or martyr.

A negative response to anger is allowing unresolved anger to become bitterness or resentment. Resentment is anger over a past injustice that is replayed over and over. Stored and stuffed, anger can, in time, become depression and/or anxiety which can steal our energy, mental and/or physical health, as well as our joy and peace.

Resentments are obsessive. They are events or situations we resend or refeel, over and over again—things we have a hard time letting go. Thus, we end up retelling the story over and over, making it worse and worse, bigger and bigger each time.

Holding a grudge is like pouring poison into a cup of coffee, hoping the other person will drink it but ending up drinking it ourselves. Resentment poisons our souls, our hearts, our minds, our behaviors, our relationships, and our lives.

When we do not resolve this anger, it stores up, building a fortress around our hearts and leaves a path of destruction in its wake. It is toxic. It must be faced and exterminated. It requires forgiveness, a deliberate act of our will, to release the power of its deadly influence. Our lives have been contaminated and consumed by it. We justify using it for our self-protection, but it doesn't save us—it ruins us!

Would you consider this an invitation to let it go? Your anger and resentment are no longer serving you or building up your life. It's hurting *you*! It's ok to let it go and let someone else fight the battle for you. You can use this energy in so many other positive and healthy ways. Consider these verses and prayers as a way to release resentment's power and let go:

> *See to it that no one comes short of the grace of God;*
> *that no root of bitterness springing up causes trouble,*
> *and by it, many be defiled.*

Hebrews 12:15

Prayer of Forgiveness

Lord, I forgive _____ for _____ .
Now please forgive me as You have promised. Forgive me for carrying
on these attitudes in my present relationships.

If we confess our sins, He is faithful and just and will
forgive us our sins and purify us from all
unrighteousness.

1 John 1:9

Prayer of Death

Lord, destroy the framework of judgment, expectancy, habits, and
attitudes in me. I take them to the cross and by the power of the cross ask
that they be put to death. I want whatever is left of me to be dead and
only You to be alive in me.

I have been crucified with Christ and I no longer live,
but Christ lives in me.

The life I live in the body, I live by faith in the Son of
God, who loved me and gave Himself for me.

Galatians 2:20

Prayer of Resurrection

Lord, reverse the old patterns in me and cause the opposite to happen. Restore to me new life, let Your life shine into all the hidden places of my heart and put a new Spirit in me.

I will give you a new heart and put a new spirit in you; I will remove from you your heart of stone and give you a heart for flesh.

Ezekiel 36:26

Biblical Insights: What Is Forgiveness?

If we want to love, we must learn how to forgive.
Mother Teresa

Forgiveness and love go hand in hand. The true meaning of forgiveness is being cleansed and freed from the impact of not only our sin but others' sins against us thanks to Jesus, who laid down His life in love and paid the price for us at the cross.

The image of the centurion, a Roman commander and soldier, kneeling at the cross portrays the power of forgiveness found in the blood of Jesus at the cross:

Because the Jews did not want bodies left on the crosses during the Sabbath, they asked Pilate to have the legs broken and the bodies were taken down ... But when they came to Jesus and found he was already dead they did not break his legs. Instead, one of the soldiers pierced Jesus' side with a spear, bringing a sudden flow of blood and water.

John 19:31–34

We all know that blood is a life-giving and life-maintaining liquid that runs through the entire body. The main job of red blood cells is to carry oxygen from the lungs to the rest of the body. Without oxygen, we do not have life; this is the life-giving part of the blood. But the red blood cell has another important job: to carry carbon dioxide as a waste product away from tissues. Blood gives life and cleanses the whole body. There's power in the blood of Jesus. His blood has both properties: life and cleansing power to wash away all our sin, iniquities and impurities.

One day as I was pondering Colossians 3:13 ("Bear with each other and forgive whatever grievances you may have against one another. Forgive, as the Lord forgave you."), I began to think about how God forgave me.

My debt to God was great. I had broken every commandment before I even knew what they were. I spent years living in depravity and debauchery, dishonoring my body and the lives of myself and others. While reflecting on my great sin problem, I received a vision.

In this vision, I saw a giant whiteboard with a list of all my wrongs, my sins, and my harms to others and myself. The board was full of descriptive, damaging words that shamefully summarized the life I had been living.

Jesus appeared in His white robe, long hair and beard, and walked lovingly and peacefully up to my whiteboard. A free-flowing fluid was running down His right arm from His hand, which held a very large sponge. It was steadily supplied with living water. He began wiping away every word, every sin, every disgusting deed I had done or would do, and every deplorable word I ever said or would say.

Effortlessly, Jesus wiped the board clean! White as snow! Not a trace of the old life was left. I was forgiven. He wiped away and removed every list of wrongs. Just like 1 Corinthians 13:4–8 says:

> *Love is patient, love is kind. It does not envy, it does not boast, it isn't proud. It isn't rude, it isn't self-seeking, it isn't easily angered.* **It keeps no record of wrongs.** *Love does not delight in evil but rejoices with the truth. It always protects, always trusts, always hopes, always perseveres. Love never fails!*

This is His promise for all His creation.

If God could do that for me, could I do the same for others? Could I, too, forgive? Forgiveness would not mean that I approved of what they did or that I would allow them to do it to me again. Neither would it be an agreement to keep or rebuild the relationship. Some people are too toxic to remain in our lives. Setting self-caring, life-giving, healthy boundaries is necessary and vital.

Forgiveness is a choice and a decision every day. It's an intentional act of my will to surrender the right to get even or pay back evil for evil. It means being willing to carry the burden of consequences of another's sin, and/or my own. It is releasing the injury into the Dead Sea and leaving it there. It's not forgetting, but letting go of the desire to relive or retrieve it in any fashion.

While my criminal record still stands to this day by the state of Colorado, my record was expunged by God and to Him, I am not a criminal, a drunk, or an addict. I am no longer ashamed, resentful, scared, and broken. To God, I always have been and always will be a perfect reflection of Him, His majestic masterpiece; worthy, wonderful and delightful just as I am. I didn't earn my worth; it was given to me before I was born. It is part of my eternal inheritance and can never be taken away.

I have a new identity and a new name. Laura comes from the root word Laurel. Laurel wreaths were given out as the trophy of victory during the Olympic Games in ancient Greece'; Laura means Victorious One. God has renamed, restored, redeemed, and reclaimed my life and story for Him to use for His purposes and glory.

He has removed our sins as far from us as the east is from the west.

Psalm 103:12 (NLT)

Chapter Eight: A Saved Majestic Masterpiece

The Spirit of the Sovereign LORD is on me, because the LORD has anointed me to proclaim good news to the poor. He has sent me to bind up the brokenhearted, to proclaim freedom for the captives and release from darkness for the prisoners, to proclaim the year of the LORD's favor and the day of vengeance of our God, to comfort all who mourn, and provide for those who grieve in Zion – —to bestow on them a crown of beauty instead of ashes, the oil of joy instead of mourning, and a garment of praise instead of a spirit of despair. They will be called oaks of righteousness, a planting of the LORD for the display of his splendor.

Isa. 61:1–3 (NIV)

Learning to Receive and Believe

Growing up, God was no more than a curse word for me. The Bible was never referred to in my home, and as far as I was concerned, God was an insignificant old dead guy. Many followers had attempted to sway me to believe, but I could not reconcile the idea of a good and loving God with the events of my past.

When I first arrived in the twelve-step rooms in 1983, something was different. The people there weren't trying to force-feed me a belief. Instead, they shared countless stories of how they came to believe in their hour of desperation. How they got on their knees and sought God honestly, humbly, and sincerely, and had a radical spiritual experience. Exactly what happened to me.

But that's as far as my faith went. I had huge trust issues and they included God. I didn't realize it at the time, but I was projecting all the traits of my earthly father onto my Heavenly Father. My dad was abandoning, punishing, cruel, hard to please, and very angry. I believed God was just the same. Men's rejection and judgment caused me to believe that God had rejected me and was judging me. I walked in fear, not faith. These beliefs were barriers to building trust with others and especially God.

Letting anyone into my life was a very slow journey. As I began to heal my shame, I embraced the idea that I was not a bad person who needed to get good, but a sick person who could get well. But God wanted more. Love and unconditional acceptance from others eventually began to win me over. Their love led me to learn more about God.

First of all, God was not like any ordinary man. He was God *and* man. What made Him different is that there was no sin in Him. He loved us perfectly and sent his blameless Son—His one and only Son—to die for us (John 3:16). Sacrificial love is an amazing characteristic of God.

But we find an even greater promise in John 3:17: "He sent his Son into the world, not to condemn the world, but to save the world through Him." He came to save, not to condemn.

The spirit of rejection is a liar, and we can see evidence of his destructive power everywhere we go. In the TV series *Free Indeed*, Pastor Robert Morris taught the seven emotions that come out of a stronghold of rejection: "a spirit of rejection: anger, insecurity, pride, independence, easily offended, excessive shyness or aloneness, fear of people and control and manipulation."

The psychological world calls this *fight, flight, freeze, or appease*. Whichever way you want to look at it, those traits are maladaptive; they're unhealthy emotions and relationship destroyers. The fact is, the Holy Spirit of God is greater than any spirit of this world, any emotional stronghold or belief.

I will pour out my Spirit on all people. Your sons and daughters will prophesy, your old men will dream dreams; your young men will see visions.

Joel 2:28

Dreams and God

A little over a year sober and clean, I had a dream. In my dream, I saw the life of Christ, from beginning to end. He was born of a virgin birth, grew and lived perfectly, loved perfectly, died on the cross, gave Himself for the sins of the world, rose again on the third day and was now alive sitting next to the Father, in heaven, praying for us.

When I woke up, I heard a voice—the voice I've come to know is God's—calmly ask, "How long have you tried to be perfect?"

I said, "My whole life, I've tried to be something someone else would like so I could be ok."

His response was sweet and simple. "I've done it for you."

My heart turned to this truth, and at that moment I came to believe that God really was who He said He was. I believed that He had sent His Son to die on the cross for my sins. I accepted the free gift, that He paid the price for my sin. I was saved at that moment. Years later, God gave me these verses to confirm my experience.

For God's will was for us to be made holy by the sacrifice of the body of Jesus Christ, once for all time. Under the old covenant, the priest stands and ministers before the altar day after day, offering the same sacrifices again and again, which can never take away sins. But our High Priest offered himself to God as a

*single sacrifice for sins, good for all time. Then sat
down in the place of honor at God's right hand. There
he waits until his enemies are humbled and made a
footstool under his feet. For by that one offering he
forever made perfect those who are being made holy.*

Hebrews 10:10–14

What I didn't know is that salvation was only the beginning
of being loved and wanted by an awesome, majestic and holy God.
I've heard it called "just accepting the fire insurance"—in other
words, just giving enough to God to keep out of hell. But God
wanted all of me. He began to unlock the places in my heart that had
been blocked by my unresolved shame and pain. He had purchased
my life and now He wanted to use me. Yet, I was still busy spending
my life on me, but fortunately, God had other plans.

Fishers of Men

Earlier that year, I had a powerful promise spoken over me. I
traveled to Miami for a large conference where thousands of
recovering people came together to celebrate the gift of recovery.

While there, I met a man who was 45 years clean and sober.
He told me his story.

He shared how, as a young man, he had been found drunk,
beat up, and a bloody mess (sounded familiar) on a street curb in
New York City. A stranger happened along and offered him a drink.
Desperate, he followed the man into an upper room, where he was
left alone with a promise of a drink upon the stranger's return.

While he waited, a group of men came into the room and
asked him what he was doing there. He told them he was waiting for

some guy to bring him a drink. The room erupted in laughter as one of the men cried out, "Son, this is where you stop drinking." Unknown to him, he was surrounded by a roomful of recovering drunks.

He responded quickly, "I can't stop drinking—I'm having too much fun!"

Again they laughed—the kind of laugh that says, "We get you! We understand!" Then one man said, "Son, how much fun can you stand?"

As the man told me his story, I laughed with him. Recovering addicts are like that. We understand the power of the disease and denial. No matter what the addiction, when we are overcome by the disease, we have a complete inability to see the truth. We are held captive by our denial, delusions, and disease.

Delusion is the story we tell ourselves that makes it ok to pick up the first one, over and over again. Denial is our complete inability to see the truth. In the twelve-step rooms, the idea that it's ok to pick up the first one despite everything we've been through is called *insanity*.

Thus the need to be "restored to sanity" as promised in the second step; the need to see the truth and not be overcome or driven by the same old lies that this time it will be different, this time it will be ok, this time it will be fun.

As I was leaving to return to my room, my new friend pulled out a fishhook pin, stuck it on my shirt and told me to go "be a fisherman of men." Flashback to my first boyfriend's death, when all that remained was the picture of Jesus and his fishing rod. Now I had a fishhook and a wonderful new vision of purpose for my life. Matthew 4:18-20, *"for they were fishermen. And he said to them, "Follow me, and I will make you fishers of men." Immediately they left their nets and followed him."*

Hitting Bottom with Codependency

After I returned from this event, I moved to Denver to pursue a new job and a new relationship. By now I was 27 years old, two years clean and sober, but I'd fallen back into my old fears and beliefs and they had taken control of my life. My life was a complete mess again.

Subconsciously I was driven by a fear that only revealed itself later. It said, "If you're not married, you'll be labeled an old maid. And if you're an old maid, you won't be worth loving." Not sure how old that generational message is, but it's pretty ancient, and it drove me right into the arms of a man who nearly took my life.

After just a few short months of dating, I convinced him to marry me. He had found a coat with my name on it and I read this as a sign from God; he was the one. I dragged him to a local church and we got married secretly. I was driven by so many underlying fears and insecurities at this time. God was there, but He was not on His throne in my life; I was still sitting there.

Within three weeks, my new husband disappeared. I searched for him frantically, to no avail. Down on my knees, I prayed. What had I done wrong? What was wrong with me? I returned to meetings, full of shock and shame, and confessed all. I was running the show alone: I had no sponsor and no recovery program.

There's much more to this story, but what's important is that a week later, my husband showed up drunk. He became progressively sicker; he was homicidal and suicidal, which eventually led both of us to be committed for treatment. The marriage was annulled within months but was really over before it began.

This was a new low for my codependency and my stubborn self-reliance— but it was the catalyst that humbled me to a deeper surrender. Good people led me to professional counseling which led me to treatment.

Right before I left, I experienced another life-changing event. On July 18, 1987, I landed in a Billy Graham Crusade in Denver, Colorado. The Mile High Stadium was packed with thousands of people. Pastor Graham's sermon was captivating, filled with love and truth that penetrated my fortress of self. My heart of stone got pierced. The message for me was loud and clear: "Laura, belief in me isn't enough. You have to commit your life to me."

The following day, my therapist sent me for 21 days to a locked-down psychiatric hospital in Largo, Florida, which facilitated a codependency treatment program. I had fallen into a suicidal depression. I was on the verge of losing my job, my relationship and marriage was a sham, my rental home had to be surrendered, and my interest in living was diminishing fast.

But I'm standing in the middle of thousands of people, listening to this man announcing that Jesus wants me. He wants me to commit my life to Him.

Defeated, I thought, "Really? You want my nothing?" And then I thought, "What do I have to lose? God couldn't possibly do anything worse to me than I've already done to myself."

Taking a leap of faith, I walked forward that night and gave up control of my shameful, broken, miserable, pathetic, damaged, lost life. Secretly I was hoping that His something would be better than my nothing. And, truth be known, my life has not been the same since.

*He can do exceedingly, abundantly beyond all that we
think, dream or imagine.*

Ephesians 3:20

God has done exceedingly and abundantly beyond all that I could think, dream or imagine, and that's what this book is all about.

I flew to Florida the next day. I began to learn about the behavioral addiction of codependency. I learned about the damaged emotions and beliefs that came from surviving trauma, sexual abuse and a parent with an addiction. They discovered I had 34 out of 35 relapse symptoms; the last one was picking up the drink and/or drug. God's rescue was right on time.

They began to open me up, exposing the secrets of my soul that had never seen the light of day. The places I had vowed no one would get in. They got in. With help, I began to unravel the lies, the shame, and the pain that had held me hostage for years.

They sent me to Adult Children of Alcoholics (ACA) meetings. I fought and argued that they were going to kill me because I believed so strongly that I needed the other meetings. Pride and ego are powerful, deadly defenses. The hospital staff refused my demands. They assured me that if I continued to hide out and look good in the other meetings, the consequences would be catastrophic.

During my first ACA meeting, I was terrified. Judgment was my constant companion. Pride said I wasn't going to learn anything from these people. Looking back now, my arrogance is shocking. I was dying on the inside and fortifying my walls to keep out the help moment by moment.

At the first meeting, the topic was self-esteem. I had no clue what self-esteem was—nor, for that matter, any clue who I was. They had me; this was the beginning of becoming teachable and humble. The experience saved my life. All the events that transpired during this time were part of God's divine plan to redeem and jump-start my healing process.

After 21 days, I returned home to a new apartment. In the middle of one quiet evening, I heard God's voice, simple and sweet:

"Restore hope to the hopeless!" I wasn't sure how or when I was going to do this, but I knew that God would show His will and His ways over time.

Restoring hope to the hopeless became my life's calling. Seeking the way of the Spirit of God has become a lifestyle, but in the beginning, it was a foreign language.

Biblical Insights: What Is Spirituality?

In the early years, I had no idea what religion and spirituality were. I had been an atheist, a nonbeliever. God was dead, if He'd ever existed in the first place.

But now I was curious. What did spirituality mean? In the dictionary, the definition of *spiritual* was "spirit-led." So I looked up *spirit*, and it said "God."

Spirituality is a God-led life. Before God, I lived a flesh-pleasing, worldly life, full of evil and twisted desires. But with God's help, I exchanged it for a Spirit-filled life, which in turn created a God-led life of blessings and love.

God lives! After His Son died on the cross, He promised to send the "comforter." He is with us always. He is personal, purposeful, powerful and intentional. There are many spirits in the world, but only one Holy Spirit powerful enough to conquer all others.

We see the Holy Spirit many times in the scriptures. He came like a dove to anoint Jesus for His ministry here on earth. When we see anointing with oil in the Bible, it's meant to rub into something the very essence of who we are, so we basically are anointed and saturated with Him. He, in turn, comes to revive, heal, empower, baptize, deliver, counsel, convict, teach, overcome, lift, carry, rejoice, lead, summon, sanctify, prophesize, praise, redeem, and restore. The list goes on and on.

These are just a few of the characteristics of the Holy Spirit of God. There are so many more. One could spend a lifetime learning and growing in the likeness of our Creator, and that is exactly what this life was intended for: learning to live out of His Spirit of love with God's companionship and help.

Biblical Insights: What Is the Exchanged Life?

The Spirit of God was deposited into my life that day. What came with it was a new sense of conviction against my pride-filled, narcissistic lifestyle. Where I once believed I had no value apart from that which men placed on me, God began to show me I had great value *in spite of* men. He began to reveal His will for me and to replace the power of pleasure-seeking with healthy conviction and respect for the things which gave me life.

All addictions—drugs, sex or approval-seeking—stop working. In recovery rooms we say, "Locked up, covered up, or sobered up." This is hitting bottom. It progresses to a point when our addictions no longer bring pleasure, but bondage and death. When we turn to God, His Holy Spirit brings conviction, which for me was an internal change of perspective. The things I thought were good were no longer good but deadly. And with conviction came a desire to do something different. Some call it a conscience or God-consciousness. I call it God getting a hold of me because He wanted so much more for me, His creation. This was not God controlling but guiding into a better plan—His best plan.

No one who is born of God will continue to sin, because
God's seed remains in him; he cannot go on sinning,
because he has been born of God.

1 John 3:9

This was the beginning of a complete transformative recovery and healing process—from mess to majestic. Years of healing work and the sanctification of the Holy Spirit of God have wiped away the generations of shame and pain. God has led me the entire way. He has always brought me exactly what I've needed when I've needed them.

Continuing to surrender and seeking to be transparent, honest, and authentic with Him and others have brought about a change in my life that I could have never produced by striving on my will power alone. His power has achieved the miraculous.

He has given me a new heart, a new spirit, and a new nature. As a believer and follower of Christ, I do not try to improve the old dead self in all its selfish, self-seeking, self-justifying ways; instead, I surrender, dying to self and continuously invite Him in to live the life only He can live through me.

Hudson Taylor, in his book *The Spiritual Secret*, said it best when he said he spent years trying to live the Christian life. He had the revelation that only Christ in him could live the Christian life.

Another face of spiritual warfare is the battle of the flesh and our sin problem. We are dead in our sin and dead to God until we are reborn of the Spirit. We can work on the physical realm all we want, but until we become alive in Christ, we are just trying to improve what is dead. It doesn't work. Idols produce dead fruit; they spoil life. Idols are the things we put ahead of God—counterfeit, self-driven solutions that do not work to solve life's greatest problems.

Yet, when I'm alive in Christ, I no longer need to put the effort into improving anything. I'm considered dead to sin and alive in Christ. Living according to the Spirit every day, listening, seeking, resting. This is the exchanged life. This is mature spiritual growth.

The most secure attachment possible is being one in Christ; I am one in Christ, therefore I am one in love. Since Christ and God are one and God is love and truth, I am already connected to the greatest source of love and truth possible.

I am crucified with Christ and I no longer live but Christ in me! (Gal. 2:20) The power of the Resurrection is unleashed to do the impossible—a new nature, a new name, a new path, a new hope—overcoming death and leading to life everlasting.

God loves us so much that He wants none before Him. This is a holy jealousy. He will break every dependency, defiance, and denial we have to bring us into the right relationship with Him. When we exchange our will for His, we share His love, power, and grace with Him and others.

This is my one purpose: to abide in Him and share His love. This isn't an easy task. Daily it is a battle with the world, the flesh, and the devil. But with God's help, all things are possible. He does not expect perfection. All He asks is that we are willing to put Him first; He'll do the rest. One of my favorite bumper stickers says, "Christians are not perfect, just forgiven."

Early on, one of the first scriptures I memorized was Matthew 6:33 (AV): "Seek ye first the kingdom of God and His righteousness, and all these things shall be added unto you."

Seek Him first, desire Him first; His will, and His face first. When I began to earnestly practice this in my life, one day at a time, an amazing supernatural life full of promises, peace, and plans for a hope and a future began to unfold before me.

Biblical Insights: The Divine Purpose of Pain

There's nothing—no circumstance, no trouble, no testing—that can ever touch me until, first of all, it has gone past God and past Christ, right through to me. If it has come that far, it has come with a great purpose, which I may not understand at the moment. But as I refuse to become panicky, as I lift up my eyes to Him and accept it as coming from the throne of God for some great purpose of blessing to my own heart, no sorrow will ever disturb me, no trial will ever disarm me, no circumstance will cause me to fret, for I shall rest in the joy of what my Lord is. That is the rest of victory.

Alan Redpath (Source Unknown)

Healing Sexual Abuse

I want to fast forward to share a story about God's timing and healing. After 12 years of recovery, my sexual abuse issues reemerged. I had tucked them neatly back into their box until an unlikely event happened that released the trigger. On that day, all my junk came up with a fury.

Connected with the injustice, I was outraged that someone had used me—a child—for their sexual pleasure. It inflamed me. Needless to say, my therapist was rejoicing, because finally, I was able to connect with the foulness of those events I had minimized in so many sessions. I had begun to feel the stinging pain of what had happened without justifying or rationalizing it away. I was enraged!

My therapist set out to teach me healthy tools for releasing my anger so it would not damage me or others. For days I cried. I punched the couch. I bounced on the trampoline until I collapsed. I vented and lamented.

God and I went to the carpet. I told Him in no uncertain terms that I wanted an explanation. Why would He allow a small child to be sexually abused? I had heard how His Son suffered as we suffered, but nowhere in the Bible did I read where Jesus experienced sexual abuse. This made me even angrier.

I approached a woman at my church who had been open about her sexual abuse. I asked her how she overcame the pain. Her response seemed glib and trite. "You just need to thank God for it."

Internally I was screaming, "Are you freaking kidding me? I will *never* thank God for this!"

Later, as I was stewing and spewing my endless "Why? Why? Why?" I heard the voice of God. "Because I love you!"

"What do you mean, you love me?"

"Laura, sex isn't the issue. Betrayal is the issue—and, yes, my Son was betrayed."

"What about rejection?"

"Yes, my Son was rejected."

"What about abandonment?"

"Yes, my Son was abandoned."

I was indignant. "What kind of God are you that you would allow your own Son to suffer this way? Are you a sadist?"

Once again, God had the perfect answer, "No! I allowed all of this because I love you. I would never force you or anyone to ever love me. These events happened in your life and my Son's life because of men who had rejected me. I would never force anyone to love me, so I gave them free will. Men without love—without Me—did the very same thing to my Son that they did to you."

Suddenly, I knew! Not only did I have a friend in Jesus, but also a comrade. He had suffered as I had suffered. The story was a little different, but the feelings were the same: shame, betrayal, rejection, and pain.

Jesus responded a little bit differently. His response was love and forgiveness: "Forgive them, Father, for they know not what they're doing." I, on the other hand, was in a full-on rage.

After about three months of madness, sharing my inconsolable pain and anger at meetings, I heard the voice of God ask me a question as I walked to my car one day. "What do you want?"

I snapped, "What do you mean, what do I want?"

Again I heard, "What do you want?"

"I want to be free to love and to be loved!"

His reply was soft and inviting. "I'm waiting."

I was a little impatient. "What are you waiting for?"

His response that day changed me forever. "All your life I have waited for you to turn to me so that I could love you!"

A *rhema* word. God speaking directly to my heart. In a moment, the rage lifted and my heart was opened; peace, love, and joy filled my soul as never before. I had been released.

The next day, a woman from my meetings approached me and asked if she could talk to me about her sexual abuse. She shared that she'd been watching me and had noticed something had happened to me; she wanted to know more about it.

We went for coffee. She shared her own story of sexual abuse, and I told her honestly that the only way I got through mine was with Jesus and a good therapist. I asked her if she knew Jesus. She said no. I asked her if she'd like to. She said yes.

Right there, she invited Jesus into her heart and life to help heal her pain. As we walked out to the car that night, these words came out of my mouth: "Isn't it amazing that my pain brought you to Him?"

Got it! Thank you, God!

In God's economy, no pain is ever wasted. My pastor heard my story and invited me to share my testimony in front of the congregation. I shared how God met me to heal the pain of my sexual abuse, but I also made my own confessions of being a user of people for my own pleasure. I shared how God's love, power, and forgiveness were the keys to setting me free. The pastor asked me, "If your perpetrator was in the audience today, could you wash his feet?"

Resoundingly and confidently I replied, "Yes, I could wash his feet. As God forgave me, I have forgiven him." Thank you, God.

Over many years now, God has used my testimony not only to save lives but to save souls for eternity. It has been an ongoing gift of my suffering and recovery that God would use my painful past to bring Him and others glory. He had an amazing plan all along.

Conclusion: Living the Promised Life

Currently I'm working towards my 35th recovery anniversary clean and sober. My husband and I have shared over 30 years of marriage and growing together in the love of the Lord. We've had our struggles but we have always kept God front and center of our relationship. Our premarital agreement was that if either of us ever raised the red flag, we'd agree to get professional help. That flag has been raised a few times over the years as we've been determined and intentional to not only heal our pain but also leave hope and a new legacy for future generations.

We have two adult children, both married, who have never seen me impaired. They have expressed gratitude on more than one occasion for being raised in a healthy, loving home where they were taught about the unfailing love of God. They know He has a perfect plan for them. He is their guide and He directs their paths for blessings and goodness, regardless of the circumstances. They and their spouses know they can call on Him for every hurt and/or problem of their lives.

My pain has been transformed into God's biggest blessing. God saw and knew the plan way before I did: that I would become a professional who specializes in healing trauma, shame, and addictions, that He would turn every part of my mess into a message and a ministry. I've been blessed to help hundreds of people as a layperson and professional.

Helping others heal and restoring hope to the hopeless while watching them come alive with the truth that they're loved has been one of the biggest blessings of my life. No matter what they've done, where they've been, or who they've hurt, God will always love and forgive them. They don't need to get good, but they can get well.

My message is simple: God's help and love are available to all who seek. Surrender to win.

I've become an advocate in my community for recovery and education. I support campaigns to stop the stigma of mental health and substance use disorders. I've been blessed to share my story to help conquer the silence and shame of addictions, sexual abuse, and trauma.

Once upon a time, I was filled with self-loathing and rage about my plight. Now, with the help of God and others, my pain has been transformed into gratitude, appreciation, and usefulness.

The very thing I hated has become my greatest gift, asset and blessing, and an opportunity to serve and help others. I thank God every day for every part of my story—even the boxes that have yet to be opened. I know the onion is still peeling.

Today, more than ever, I want to witness to the world that God loves us. He is there for us. He desires us. Recovery and healing are possible. Turn to Him. He's waiting for you with open arms—no matter what!

In this life, we will be given way more than we can handle. That's the nature of life. But our loving Father can handle every problem of our lives if we trust and lean on Him. He will not only give you a new heart but bless you with an amazing life. I pray you will turn and seek Him, so you too can experience His love for you.

> *Then you will call on me and come and pray to me, and*
> *I will listen to you. You will seek me and find me when*
> *you seek me with all your heart. I will be found by you,*
> *declares the Lord, and will bring you back from*
> *captivity …*

Jeremiah 29:12–14a

The Old Is Gone. The New Has Come!

In April 2019, I planned a ski trip, returning to the place where my life crashed and burned back in 1985. The front cover of my Daily

Bread Devotional said this: "If anyone is in Christ, the new creation has come." (2 Cor. 5:17).

As I prepared for my trip, I wondered whether the healing work accomplished over the years would be enough. Would I really experience complete liberation from pain as I walked through the town where building after building would remind me of my life before God? A time when I had experienced so much loss, violence, loneliness, depression, incarceration, and shame. A place where my appetite for excesses was a way of life; when drunkenness, drugs, lust, and the spiral of self-loathing and shame made a downward staircase to validate my unworthiness.

Back then, I had been living in false happiness, believing the counterfeits, the false idols would satisfy me; I now know it was all a lie. What feelings would surface? Was I healed enough? Would I walk the streets in peace and joy, or painful contemplation?

As I drove into town, I saw the old familiar places. There was my first apartment, then the old cabin, bringing memories of happy times, my expected arrival after the long drive from Washington to Colorado. Remembering, reminiscing, and reconnecting with old friends. It had been an exciting time.

Moving through town, I noticed the old haunts were gone. The familiar old buildings were still there, but new businesses inhabited them. Everything was new and different. Multiple stoplights where there had been just one, five peaks to ski where there had been just two. A new town came into view. Checking in with myself, there was no pain; memories galore, but no pain.

My old address clung to my memory like a piece of gum stuck to my shoe. The house had been a quaint, weathered A-frame. As I drove around the familiar bend in the road just before the driveway, I did not see the A-frame. I made a U-turn. Instead of the

A-frame, there was a beautiful modern mountain home, luxurious, grand and brand new.

I was filled with joy and excitement. The metaphor God had prepared for me was simple. "This is your life. The old is gone, the new has come." A *rhema* word. Nothing in this town resembled what I had known. It was completely new, and so was I.

Once again, I was reminded that healing isn't forgetting, but feeling with less pain; here I was, standing in historically one of the most painful places of my life, feeling joy and relief.

The depth of my brokenness that was healed is the depth of the compassion given. God has been cleaning my internal house to make more room for Him—His love, His grace, His mercy—to pour out for others. The old is gone. The new has come!

Grace and favor followed me for the rest of the week.

My childhood ski buddies endured many nights of my drama during my using years. In recovery, I reached out to them to make amends afraid that they would want nothing to do with me. Instead, I was greeted with concern, grace and forgiveness, wonderful gifts of loving friends.

Here it was years later, and I got a beautiful invitation to meet up for some runs. It was a happy reunion on a perfect bluebird day. The air was crisp. Snow-covered peaks surrounded every run. We headed to the top of the world and skied double black diamond runs like carefree eagles, soaring. My joy was complete in freedom, fellowship, and fun that day. Free to live, love, and be loved again.

My ski buddies achieved their dreams of becoming top-notch ski professionals. For years I marveled at their pictures posted from around the world, especially training photos taken at the Zermatt Matterhorn Glacier in Switzerland. It seemed only fitting that this would be the cover to my first book.

There are so many promises in God's word that have come true for me. My life is a radiant reflection of the One who loves me. He healed all my misery and spared my life from death. He saved me from an eternity of hell and redeemed every part of my past as an expression and extension of His love. Then He turned around and used every part of my past for His purposes.

I am a new creation. Love, joy, peace, and gratitude fill the old cracks in my heart. I will continue to boast of my weaknesses that I may reflect His power. Today, I can comfort others as God has comforted me. His word has become the compass of truth for my life. He has consoled me with His love. I've been restored, renewed, and redeemed: Mess to Majestic.

"I pray that out of his glorious riches he may strengthen you with power through His Spirit in your inner being, so that Christ may dwell in your hearts through faith. And I pray that you, being rooted and established in love, may have power, together with all the Lord's holy people, to grasp how wide and long and high and deep is the love of Christ and to know this love that surpasses all knowledge - that you may be filled to the measure of all the fullness of God. Now to him who can do immeasurably more than all we ask or imagine, according to his power that is at work within us, to him be glory in the church and in Christ Jesus throughout all generations, forever and ever! Amen " (Eph 16-21).

Bibliography

All scriptures were taken from the NIV version of the Bible unless otherwise noted.

Chapter 1

Al-Anon Family Groups. (ND). *Opening our Hearts, Transforming our Losses.* Virginia Beach: Al-Anon Family Groups Headquarters, Inc.

Alcoholics Anonymous World Services Inc. (1967). *As Bill Sees It.* New York: Alcoholics Anonymous World Services, Inc.

Chapter 2

Evans, J. (ND). *When Life Hurts.* Amarillo, TX.

Kubler-Ross, D. E. (2019). *Stage of Grief Models Kubler Ross.* Retrieved from http://mentalhelp.net: http://mentalhelp.net/grief-and-bereavement/stage-of-grief-models-kubler-ross/

Manning, B. (2002). *Ruthless Trust.* New York: HarperCollins.

Scazzero, P. (2017). *Emotionally Healthy Relationships Day by Day.* Grand Rapids: Zondervan.

Chapter 3

Alcoholics Anonymous World Services, Inc. (2001). *Alcoholics Anonymous*. New York City: Alcoholics Anonymous World Services, Inc.

Dayton, T. M. (2012, December). The ACoA Trauma Syndrome. *Counselor Magazine*, pp. 37-42.

Gilliver, C. (2018). Trauma-Informed Care in Response to Adverse Childhood Experiences. *Nursing Times*, 114:7, 46-49.

Hammond, D. (Director). (2020). *Cracked Up* [Motion Picture].

Hinrichs J, D. J. (2011). Personality subtypes in adolescent and adult children of alcoholics; a two part study. *J Nerv Mental Disorders*, 199(7);487-98.

James G. Friesen, P. E. (2000-R). *Living from the Heart Jesus Gave You*. Pasadena: Shepherd's House Inc.

Jane Evans, S. M. (2019, ND). *tohavehope.com*. Retrieved from Helping Adoptive and Foster Families Get to Happy & Healthy : tohavehope.com

Kolk, D. B. (2019). Childhood Trauma Leads to Brains Wired for Fear. (B. Lewis, Interviewer)

Woititz, J. E. (ND). *Adult Children of Alcoholics*. MN: Hazelden .

Woititz, J. G. (n.d.). *Lifeskills for Adult Children*. Amazon.

Chapter 4

Alcoholics Anonymous World Services, Inc. (2001). *Alcoholics Anonymous*. New York City:
    Alcoholics Anonymous World Services, Inc.

Lane, Daniel V. JD, C. I.-M. (2006, December 31). *Recovery and the Law Part II*. Retrieved from anonymousone.com:
    www.anonymousone.com/faq74.htm

Lieber, C. Y. (1975). The Effect of Chronic Ethanol Consumption on Acetaldehyde Metabolism. *Helsinki: Finnish Foundation for Alcohol Studies*, 83–104.

Ohlms, D. L. (1983). *The Disease Concept of Alcoholism*. Belleville: Gary Whiteaker Company.

Schuckit, M. A. (1979). Ethanol Ingestion Differences in Blood Acetaldehyde Concentrations in Relatives of Alcoholics and Controls. *Science*, 54.

Ventimiglia, M. (Director). (2019). *This is Us* [Motion Picture].

Wikipedia. (2020, January 8). *https://en.wikipedia.org/wiki/Caffeine*. Retrieved from wikipedia.org:
    https://en.wikipedia.org/wiki/Caffeine

Chapter 5

Abrams, J. (Director). (2019). *Star Wars: The Rise of Skywalker* [Motion Picture].

Bourdain, A. (2017, January 15). Observer Food Monthly. (J. Hind, Interviewer)

Bradshaw, J. (1988). *Bradshaw on: The Family.* Deerfield Beach: Health Communications, Inc.

Bradshaw, J. (1990). Overcoming Toxic Shame. *VHS.* Unknown.

Brene Brown Phd., L. (2016). Shame Shields, Webinar.

Dayton, T. M. (2012, December). The ACoA Trauma Syndrome. *Counselor Magazine,* pp. 37–42.

Evans, J. (ND). Fight for your Mind. Amarillo, TX.

Savard, L. (1992). *Shattering Your Strongholds.* Gainsville: Bridge-Logos.

Scazzero, P. and. (2017). *Emotionally Healthy Relationships.* Grand Rapids: Zondervan.

Chapter 6

Lively, Pastor Rich, (2019) First Baptist Church of Cocoa, November 10, 2019 Sermon notes, Cocoa, Florida

Eldridge, J. (2001). *Wild at Heart.* Nashville: Thomas Nelson.

Manning, B. (2000). *Ruthless Trust - The Ragamuffin's Path to God.* New York: HarperCollins.

Chapter 7

Recommended Reading: Neil T. Anderson, bestselling author of *Victory Over the Darkness*, *The Bondage Breaker*, and *The Steps to Freedom In Christ*, published by Bethany House Publishers. www.bethanyhouse.com

Chapter 8

Recommended Reading: The Bible, God's word, in any translation. His love story to you!

About the Author

 Laura McCarthy began her personal recovery and healing from substance use disorders, trauma, shame and co-dependency on May 3, 1985.

She has a passion to stop the stigma, restore hope to the hopeless, and share the love of God. She loves to witness to the power of a loving God, educate, inspire and motivate others into their own healing and recovery.

To fulfill her passion, she became a Licensed Mental Health Counselor (LMHC) and Masters Certified Addictions Professional (MCAP) in her home state.

Laura is a Certified Biblical Counselor and member of the American Association of Christian Counselors (AACC) since 2001 as well as a follower of Jesus Christ since July 18, 1987.

Considered an expert in addictions, she is the founder of Brevard Opioid and Addictions Conference held every September in honor of National Recovery Month. She is an active member of her home church.

She is EMDR trained and a member of the Space Coast Mental Health Counselors Association (SCMHCA), and the local Prevention Coalition, and Brevard Opioid Abuse Task Force.

She has been married to her husband for over 30 years, and has two adult children. They reside in the Space Coast of Florida.

Thank You For Reading My Book!

Can You Help?

I really appreciate all your feedback and I love hearing what you have to say.

I need your input to make the next version of this book and my future books better.

Please leave me an honest review on Amazon letting me know what you thought of the book.

You can also visit me on my website at

www.LauraMcCarthyAuthor.com

Thanks so much!

Laura McCarthy, MA, LMHC, MCAP

NOW IT'S YOUR TURN

**Discover the EXACT three-step blueprint you need to become
a bestselling author in three months.**

Self-Publishing School helped me, and now I want them to help you.
Even if you're busy, bad at writing, or don't know where to start,
you CAN write a bestseller and build your best life.

With tools and experience across a variety of niches and professions,

Self-Publishing School can help you take your book to the finish line!

DON'T WAIT

EMAIL ME TODAY AT

MESSTOMAJESTICBOOK@GMAIL.COM

Made in the USA
Middletown, DE
25 May 2020